CAREER
CLUES FOR THE CLUELESS

CHRISTOPHER D. HUDSON
DENISE KOHLMEYER
RANDY SOUTHERN

PROMISE
PRESS
An Imprint of Barbour Publishing

Career Clues for the Clueless
Copyright 1999 by Promise Press, an imprint of Barbour Publishing, Inc. All rights reserved.

Check out Barbour's exciting web site at: http://www.barbourbooks.com

Developed and produced by the Livingstone Corporation.

Interior Design by Design Corps, Batavia, IL.

Cover Design by Robyn Martins.

Cover and Interior Artwork by Elwood Smith.

ISBN: 1-57748-492-4

Published by: Promise Press, an imprint of Barbour Publishing, Inc., P.O. Box 719
                  Uhrichsville, OH   44683.

Printed in the United States of America.

TABLE OF CONTENTS

SECTION 1
CHOOSING A CAREER 1

SECTION 2
FINDING A JOB 27

SECTION 3
KEEPING A JOB 101

SECTION 4
OVERVIEW OF JOBS 153

INTRODUCTION

"You want sausage with that?"
"You want that in Large, XL, or XXL?"
"You want it in blue or green?"

Unfortunately, not all decisions are that easy. There are even a few times in life when we have to make a really BIG decision. This may be one of those times for you. What should you do? What kind of job are you best suited for? How much do you need to make? Where should you apply? Questions like these probably swirl through your head.

Is there hope? Yes. Is it possible for you to find a job that will pay you enough *and* that you'll enjoy? Yes. What, don't you agree?

Perhaps you've heard that it's impossible. Perhaps you've hated enough jobs and known enough people who have lived for the weekend to convince you that work will never be fun, enjoyable, or challenging.

Wrong on all counts. While you'll never have a job that doesn't take effort, you don't have to dread your job. You can find a job that fits your personality and talents, pays you enough, and gives you fulfillment. All you need to do is to learn a little about yourself and the market. This book is the place to start. Here's what you'll find between the covers:

CATCH A CLUE

A Truckload of Clues. You'll learn tips from people who have successfully navigated their careers. They've learned a lot about getting the most out of them. While they've learned some of it the hard way, it's all here so you don't have to.

WIDE ANGLE

Perspective. Sometimes we get caught up in details of our jobs and decision making. To make the best decision, though, we need help looking at the whole picture. We'll help you take a step back.

WOW!

Humorous stories and Incredible facts. Every job has a lighter side. We've collected some of the best stories for you to enjoy.

DON'T FORGET

Important Reminders. Certain things are important to remember if you plan on succeeding in your quest for the perfect job. We've highlighted those for you.

THE BOTTOM LINE

The Bottom Line. We'll help you get beyond confusion by letting you know the most important stuff to remember.

THE BIBLE SAYS

Help from Above. We've highlighted a few key Bible verses that will encourage you in your job search and your career planning.

Work will always be work, but it doesn't have to be drudgery. Picking the right job for the right company and for the right reasons can lead you to the best job for you. So, before you check out one more job or make any more plans, there's one critical thing you need to do: *read this book*. Feel free to read it *your* way: from cover to cover or skipping around to the parts that interest you most. No matter how you read it, you'll find it's jammed with good advice, great ideas and funny stories. So turn the page and start reading. . . . You'll be glad you did!

SECTION 1

CHOOSING A CAREER

HOLY JOB SEARCH!

A CHRISTIAN APPROACH TO CAREER PLANNING

"Whatever you do, do it all for the glory of God" (1 Corinthians 10:31).
This is the principle that guides all career matters for God's people. Whether you're a brain surgeon, a librarian, a systems analyst, or a photographer, you have a responsibility to use your career to bring glory to the Lord. But beyond this basic principle, the Bible has much to say about Christians and work.

PART OF THE PLAN

Our Heavenly Father happens to be a big fan of work. In fact, he created us with a natural capacity for it. Genesis 2:15 says God put Adam in the Garden of Eden "to work it and take care of it." God's plan for Adam holds true for us today. We were made to work.

Psalm 90:17 offers another incentive for labor. The verse suggests that work allows us to leave our mark on society. When a person's labor is blessed by the Lord, it becomes a lasting legacy, a testimony to the worker.

What's more, verses like Proverbs 10:4 and 14:23 equate hard work with wealth—if not material riches, then spiritual ones, the kind that really matter.

ALL WORK AND NO PLAY MAKES JACK . . . AN IDOLATER?

"You shall have no other gods before me" (Exodus 20:3).

"Keep yourselves from idols" (1 John 5:21).

To some people, these might seem like the easiest commandments in the Bible to obey. Let's face it: bowing down to a carved statue isn't real high on the list of modern temptations. But what if we defined *other gods* or *idols* as anything in our lives that is given higher priority than the Lord?

Hmmm. Let's talk about careers, shall we?

Careers matter in our society. (If they didn't, would you be looking for one right now?) Ever notice how often people allow themselves to be defined by what they do for a living?

- "My name's Sharon. I'm a sales rep for Carson Pirie Scott."
- "My mother will be happy when she hears I'm dating a doctor."
- "Now entering the studio are today's contestants: a high school science teacher from Akron, Ohio . . ."

Don't allow yourself to be defined by your career. And don't allow your career to become an idol. You may be surprised at how easily a job can dominate your life, if you allow it to. Keep in mind that your career is a means for glorifying God and fulfilling his will in your life. A career should be a priority in your life, but never your highest priority.

DON'T LIMIT YOUR OPTIONS

There's no reason to think you have to become a pastor or Sunday school teacher or missionary to be used by the Lord. God works through people

WOW!

Second Careers?

Is it possible that some of the most famous people in the Bible actually missed their true vocational callings? Take a look at some of the alternate career choices we've come up with for some of your favorite Bible characters. Like all self-respecting career planners, we based our recommendations on each person's specific skills and characteristics.

Person	Skill/Characteristic	Alternate Career Option
Noah	Spent over a year inside a gigantic enclosed boat, caring for every species of animal on Earth.	Sanitation engineer
Abraham	Haggled with God about how many righteous people in Sodom it would take for God to spare the city.	Union labor negotiator
Jacob	Talked his brother Esau into trading his birthright for a bowl of stew.	Used car salesman
Moses	Led millions of Israelites from Egypt to the Promised Land.	Travel agent
Joshua	Led the attack against Jericho in which the Israelites knocked down the walls of the city simply by blowing horns.	Band leader

Person	Skill/Characteristic	Alternate Career Option
Daniel	Spent the night in a den of hungry lions without being eaten.	Circus performer
Shadrach, Meshach, and Abednego	Survived being thrown into a fiery oven; walked around in the flames without even getting their clothes singed.	Furnace repairmen
Jonah	Stayed alive for three days in the belly of a giant fish.	Marine biologist
John	Raced to Jesus' tomb as fast as he could when he heard that Jesus' body was gone.	Investigative journalist
Thomas	Refused to believe that Jesus rose from the dead without physical proof.	Judge

in all walks of life to accomplish His will. All that's needed is a willing spirit.

The apostle Peter was a fisherman, and look what God did through him! Paul was tent maker. Luke was a doctor. Matthew was a tax collector, for crying out loud! In New Testament times, tax collectors were every bit as respected as sleazy lawyers are today. Yet God used all of these people in ways they could not imagine. Who's to say he won't do the same through your career—whatever that career may be!

LOOK BEFORE YOU LEAP

DISCOVERING WHAT YOU NEED IN A CAREER

Ken attended Bowling Green University on an athletic scholarship. Soccer had always been his main passion in life, so when the time came to choose a major, Ken wasn't sure what he wanted to do. He'd always enjoyed science classes in high school, so he started taking some general biology courses. From there, he narrowed his interest to the field of microbiology. During the first semester of his sophomore year, Ken declared a microbiology major.

From that point on, Ken pursued soccer and science with equal zeal. He posted solid, if not spectacular, grades in his core courses. He graduated with honors and a bachelor of science degree.

Eager to complete his education, Ken applied for a program at Loyola University that would allow him to earn both his master's degree and his doctorate in three years. He was accepted.

Ken's first two years at Loyola were eye-opening to say the least. Hundreds of hours in the lab, peering into test tubes, checking and rechecking calculations, gave him his first real taste of a scientist's life. Much to his dismay, Ken found that he didn't care for it much.

Yet, he pressed on. For his doctoral work, he labored for months on an experiment involving fruit flies. Ultimately, the experiment failed, souring Ken even further to the fickle nature of scientific research. Ken managed to churn out a dissertation on his failed experiment and successfully defend it, thus earning his doctorate.

Despite his experiment's failure, Ken landed a post-doctorate position at one of the most prestigious research firms in the Midwest. Ken's future seemed assured. But on the first day of his post-doctorate work, reality smacked Ken upside the head. He looked around the sterile, solitary environment of the laboratory and realized that he needed something more: human interaction. Perhaps a little late, Ken decided that he wanted to work with people, not test tubes. He still wanted to pursue science, but not in a laboratory.

So Ken went back to school for two more years to get a teaching certificate. He is now a high school science teacher who loves his job. Incidentally, he was also able to incorporate his other passion in life into his career. Ken serves as an assistant coach for the high school soccer team.

What can you learn from Ken's experience?

KNOW WHAT YOU NEED IN A CAREER

Careers can be divided into four categories.

1. Working with people. This would include everything from sales to entertainment. Guidance counselors, therapists, teachers, and coaches all fall within this category.

2. Working with information. Scientists, accountants, computer programmers, and stockbrokers can all be grouped in this category.

3. Working with words. Obviously this category would include authors, editors, and newspaper journalists.

4. Working with objects. Perhaps the most diverse of the categories, this would include everyone from sculptors to auto mechanics. Plumbers, machinists, and chefs also fit here.

In order to find a truly fulfilling career, you'll need to decide which of these job types is most appealing to you. Think of the time and energy Ken wasted as a result of skipping this step. If he'd identified his need to work with people early in his decision-making process, he never would have pursued a career in laboratory research.

One more thing: Don't assume that these categories are mutually exclusive. Many careers are "hybrids," combining two or more different categories. Teaching, for example, involves working with both people and information.

The Bible and Your Career Decision

THE BIBLE SAYS   *God cares about your decisions.*

The Bible says:
"A person's steps are directed by the Lord, and the Lord delights in his way" (Psalm 37:23, God's Word).

SPEND SOME TIME ON THE JOB

If Ken had been able to actually observe what research scientists do all day, he may have realized much earlier in his career search that a laboratory setting was no place for him.

If you'd like to guard against "career regret," you might want to consider scheduling a "tag-along" appointment to find out all you can about the career you're considering. Here's what you'll need to do:

1. Get the name of someone who is working in the field of your choice. It may be a person you know from church, a neighbor, a friend of your parents, or a casual acquaintance of your second cousin. It doesn't matter how you get the name, just find someone!

2. Beg, bribe, or threaten the person until he or she agrees to "guide" you through a day of work. Or, if those tactics don't work, simply explain your reason for wanting to tag along. Keep in mind that you'll need to give the person plenty of time to make the necessary arrangements for your visit. You may also need to convince the person that you're not going to do anything stupid or embarrassing in his or her workplace.

3. Prepare for your tag-along day as you would for a job interview. Dress and behave in a professional manner. Be polite and respectful with everyone you meet. In short, act like you belong in the workplace!

4. Ask every job-related question that pops into your head. Don't be obnoxious about it, but if you're unclear about something you see in the workplace, ask your "guide" to explain it to you. The whole purpose of the tag-along day is to find out as much as you can about the job. Don't squander the experience simply because you're afraid to ask a question.

5. Do something nice to show your appreciation to your guide. Take him or her out to lunch. Send a thank-you card and a small gift. Above all, stay in contact with this person. He or she may turn out to be a valuable resource when you start looking for a job!

DON'T BE AFRAID TO ADMIT AND CORRECT A MISGUIDED CAREER CHOICE

Ken took a lot of flak for his decision to give up research for a career in teaching. His parents were disappointed and his friends laughed. Yet Ken was undeterred. Today no one's laughing at his decision. You see, Ken may have become a pretty good researcher, but he's an *outstanding* science teacher! More importantly, he's a *fulfilled* science teacher.

    If you find yourself on a career path that feels like a mistake to you, find

WOW!

Jobs You Won't Find on Any Résumé

If you ever decide to change careers, you'll find yourself in some pretty famous company. We all know Ronald Reagan was an actor before he became president. But you may be surprised at some of the former careers of other well-known people.

This Person ...	Was Once a ...
Dan Aykroyd	Postal worker
Sean Connery	Milkman
Elvis Costello	Computer programmer
Danny DeVito	Hairdresser
Whoopi Goldberg	Make-up artist for corpses
Adolf Hitler	Painter
Dustin Hoffman	Waiter
L. Ron Hubbard	Science fiction novelist
Steve Martin	Vendor at Disneyland
Geraldo Rivera	Lawyer
Sylvester Stallone	Gym teacher
Rod Stewart	Grave digger

a new path. Don't allow outside pressures to force you into a career you don't want. Admit your mistake and take the necessary steps to correct it. In the end, you—and everyone who cares about you—will be glad you did.

GRABBING FOR THE GREEN

HOW IMPORTANT IS MONEY IN MY CAREER DECISION?

Cash, moolah, dead presidents, benjamins—call it what you want, but if you're considering a career, sooner or later you're going to have to think about money. After all, money's the whole point of working, isn't it?

Not by a long shot.

In fact, if you choose a job based solely on how much money you'll make, you can say "buh-bye" to your chances for a truly fulfilling career, not to mention a God-honoring life. Think we're exaggerating? Check out what God has to say about money in his Word.

> "Whoever loves money never has money enough; whoever loves wealth is never satisfied with his income" (Ecclesiastes 5:10).

> "No one can serve two masters. Either he will hate the one and love the other, or he will be devoted to the one and despise the other. You cannot serve both God and Money" (Matthew 6:24).

Earning money isn't evil. Earning *a lot* of money isn't evil. But making money the number one priority in your life *is* evil—and it leads to all kinds of trouble.

Don't let dollar signs cloud your career vision. Remember, money is just one of many factors to consider when choosing a career.

WHAT OTHER THINGS SHOULD I CONSIDER IN CHOOSING A CAREER?

For a truly fulfilling work experience, there are factors other than money that you should weigh. Here are some questions you should ask yourself as you search for your ideal career.

- Does this job allow me to use my God-given gifts and abilities?
- Is it work that I can be proud of?
- Does it challenge me intellectually?
- Will it put me in contact with potential mentors and teachers?
- Does it offer recognition for outstanding work?
- Does it provide a worker-friendly environment?
- Does it provide opportunities to work independently?

If you're considering a specific organization, narrow your questions further.

- Will I be working with people I respect and get along with?
- Does my boss's personality suit mine?
- Does this company produce quality products or service?
- Does it have a good reputation in the industry?
- Is it committed to improvement?
- Does it offer health insurance, continuing-education, or other benefits I need?
- Is there anything about the company's practices that disturbs me?
- Does the company promote from within?
- Does it encourage professional growth?

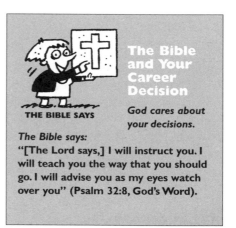

THE BIBLE SAYS

The Bible and Your Career Decision

God cares about your decisions.

The Bible says:
"[The Lord says,] I will instruct you. I will teach you the way that you should go. I will advise you as my eyes watch over you" (Psalm 32:8, God's Word).

MAKING ENDS MEET

HOW MUCH MONEY DO YOU NEED?

Before you start talking about financial intake, you should probably take a hard look at what your monthly *output* will be. How much will it cost you to maintain at least a decent standard of living? What bills do you need to factor into your budget? In other words, what's the minimum amount of money you need in order to live each month?

Below we've listed several possible monthly expenditures for you to consider. Only when you've taken all of them into account can you start thinking about your salary requirements.

Tithing
What percentage of your income will you be giving back to the Lord?

Rent
Will you be sharing an apartment with one or more roommates to cut down on expenses? Will you be living at home with your parents?

Utilities
How much will you be paying for electricity, gas, and water? How high will your phone bills be? Do you need cable TV?

Food
Will you be buying groceries or eating out most of the time?

Car
Are you making payments on your vehicle?

Maintenance
How much money will you need to put away each month in order to cover tune-ups, oil changes, and unexpected repairs?

Commute
If you plan to drive to work, how much will you be paying for gas? If you plan to take public transportation, how much will you be paying for bus or train tickets?

Insurance
How much will you be paying for auto insurance? Will your apartment complex require you to purchase renter's insurance? Do you have life insurance payments to consider?

School loans
How much money will you be repaying each month?

Credit cards
What bills are you trying to pay off?

Wardrobe
Will your job require you to regularly purchase expensive clothing?

Spending cash
How often do you buy CDs, rent movies, golf, or attend concerts? How much money do you spend each month on hobbies?

Total up the numbers for each category. The sum you arrive at is the absolute minimum you'll need to survive each month. When you're in salary negotiations, keep this number in mind as the very lowest offer you can afford to accept.

TESTING, TESTING

WHICH CAREERS ARE BEST FOR YOU

With hundreds of thousands of career options available, you may be asking, "Where do I begin?" Strange as it may sound, the best place to start is with yourself. How well do you know yourself? How much time have you spent thinking about your likes and dislikes, your talents and weaknesses, the things that are most important to you?

These factors are extremely important in choosing a career. That's why over the years dozens of tests and resources have been created to help people identify vital characteristics of their personalities and then match those characteristics with potential careers. If you're serious about finding a career, you may want to investigate some of the following resources.

THE MEYERS-BRIGGS TYPE INDICATOR

Though it's not specifically a career test, the Meyers-Briggs Type Indicator (known simply as MBTI to its friends) can be a valuable tool for someone looking for career direction.

The MBTI is a personality type test. The theory behind the test can be broken down into four statements.

1. A person is either primarily introverted (I) or extroverted (E).
Introverted people think best alone, processing ideas in their own minds. Extroverted people are energized by contact with people, preferring to discuss ideas with others.

2. A person is either primarily sensing (S) or intuitive (N).
Sensing people trust what they see, hear, smell, taste, and touch. Intuitive people rely on instincts.

3. A person is either primarily thinking (T) or feeling (F).
Thinking people make choices based on logic and objectivity. Feeling people make decisions based on their own personal value system.

4. A person is either primarily judging (J) or perceiving (P).
Judging people prefer organization, closure, and structured environ-

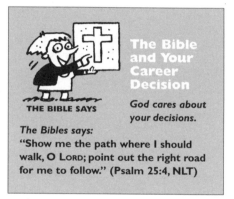

The Bible and Your Career Decision

THE BIBLE SAYS

God cares about your decisions.

The Bibles says:
"Show me the path where I should walk, O LORD; point out the right road for me to follow." (Psalm 25:4, NLT)

ments. Perceiving people prefer flexibility, diversity, and casual environments.

The test itself is a series of questions based on personal preferences. (Forget trying to study for this baby; there are no right or wrong answers.) Your personality type is determined by your responses. After the test is evaluated, you're given a letter code that indicates your preference in each category. (For example, INTJ is introverted, intuitive, thinking, and judging; ESFP is extroverted, sensing, thinking, and judging; and PB&J is best served on white bread.)

Identifying and exploring your natural preferences can teach you a great deal about your strengths and weaknesses—why some things come so easily to you while others present more of a challenge. When you apply that knowledge to a career search, you get a better sense of the work environment you'd be most comfortable in, the tasks you're best suited for, and the people with whom you'd be most productive.

The MBTI's not going to tell you what career would be best for you, but it may tell you things about yourself that will make your career choice a little more obvious.

(If you'd like more information on the Meyers-Briggs Type Indicator, check out the organization's web site at http://www.meyers-briggs.com.*)*

THE STRONG INTEREST INVENTORY

The Strong Interest Inventory is used to help people understand their work preferences and direct them to occupations in which they probably would be most comfortable. Like the MBTI, the Strong is not a test of abilities; it's an inventory of interests.

The Strong Interest Inventory can help a job seeker
- explore a range of career alternatives,
- narrow career choices to a few possibilities,
- discover new and exciting career options, or
- confirm a career choice that's already been made.

During the evaluation of the test, each person's responses are compared with answers given by people already working in a wide variety of jobs. The person's score, then, shows how similar his or her interests are to the interests of people in different fields. This information can be quite valuable in determining a career path.

(If you'd like more information on the Strong Interest Inventory, check with your local college career center.)

THE CAMPBELL INTEREST AND SKILL SURVEY

As its name implies, the Campbell Interest and Skill Survey is a career planning tool that measures a person's interests and skills. The interest scale of the survey gauges the person's attraction for specific occupational areas. The skill scale estimates the person's confidence in his or her ability to perform various occupational activities.

Be warned: The Campbell Survey focuses specifically on careers that require a higher education. The test is most useful for people who have completed college, people who are currently attending college, or people who plan to attend college.

(If you'd like more information on the Campbell Interest and Skill Survey, check with your local college career center.)

GOT MONEY TO BURN?

Some companies offer career testing services on a much more personal (and much more expensive) basis. For example, the Johnson O'Connor Institute, which has branches in most major American cities, offers its career assessment services for a fee of $480 (call 1-800-452-1539). Don't feel like leaving the house to assess your career? Call the people at the Rockport Institute (301-340-6600), and they'll conduct an interest test and offer an evaluation over the phone—all for $450.

While these tests may seem quite expensive, they're also quite thorough. The results you receive will be extremely helpful as you make your way through the maze of career choices.

IF MONEY'S TIGHT

All of the tests, inventories, and surveys we've listed so far cost money. Some are pretty expensive. If you're looking for a cheap alternative, head for the nearest decent-sized public library you can find. Ask the librarian to direct you to the career resource section. There you'll find dozens of books, magazines, and newsletters designed to help you match your skills and interests with potential careers.

A little something extra: Because you seem like such a nice person, we'll even start you off with three titles to look for at the library.

- *The Enhanced Guide to Occupational Exploration*
- *The Dictionary of Occupational Titles*
- *The Occupational Outlook Handbook*

You probably got bored just reading the titles of these books. But trust us, if you're looking for a career, these are the resources you want in your hands. Crack them open, and you'll find more information than you ever imagined about hundreds and hundreds of careers. The more you explore these and other resources, the better chance you'll have of finding the career that best suits your needs and talents.

THE MOST IMPORTANT TEST OF ALL

The Meyers-Briggs Indicator, the Strong Inventory, and the Campbell Survey are all helpful resources, but if you're seriously contemplating your career path, one test is absolutely *essential.* It's only one question long, but that one question may take a while to answer. And believe me, you don't want to rush your response.

If you've got your #2 pencil and blue notebook ready, here's the question:

What does the Lord have planned for your life?

Any answers spring to mind right away? If so, write 'em down. If not, don't worry. Most people have trouble answering that question at first. If you need some help, here's a simple four-step method you might try.

The Bible and Your Career Decision

THE BIBLE SAYS

God cares about your decisions.

The Bible says:
"I know the plans I have for you, declares the LORD. They are plans for peace and not disaster, plans to give you a future filled with hope" (Jeremiah 29:11, God's Word).

1. Examine yourself.
Make a list of the gifts and abilities you think God has given you. This is no time for false modesty. If you believe God has blessed you with a talent or personality trait, write it down.

2. Pray.
Ask God to serve as your career guidance counselor. Ask Him to remind you of any other gifts or talents you forgot to include on your list. Then ask Him

to guide you as you research careers in which you can put your unique abilities to work.

3. See what Scripture says.

Unless you've got a really weird version of the Bible, you're not going to find verses that say, "Thou shalt design software for home schooling programs" or "Blessed are the accountants, for they shall inherit unbelievable retirement benefits." But you *will* find principles to guide you as you make the tough career decisions that lie ahead. Using a Bible concordance, see what God's Word has to say about things like money, work, and honoring the Lord in all you do.

4. Seek the advice of others.

Talk to some respected, mature Christian friends and acquaintances. See if they have any opinions as to how you might best use your God-given abilities. You may be surprised to find out that some of these people already have you pictured in certain careers!

A Final Word

Don't make the career testing process any longer or more involved than it needs to be. If you know yourself at all, you can probably name at least a couple of careers that you're well-suited for. You can also probably name a few careers that have always seemed interesting to you. That's a great place to start! While some career tests may suggest a couple of off-the-wall jobs that you would never have thought of in a million years, for the most part, they usually affirm what you already know. After all, some things are obvious. If you're scared of dogs, cats, and horses, a veterinary career is probably not in the cards for you. If your watercolors have taken first-place three years in a row at the county craft fair, you might consider a career in art. In other words, don't be afraid to dream and explore when it comes to your career, but also don't lose sight of the obvious.

WHAT'S HOT? WHAT'S NOT?

CAREER AND EMPLOYMENT PROJECTIONS FOR THE TWENTY-FIRST CENTURY

What you'll find here are several lists of careers that are projected to be "hot" in the next millennium. Career and employment experts compile these lists to give college students and beginning job seekers an idea of which fields they might want to pursue. The reasoning is that if a field or industry is projected to grow throughout the next decade or two, it's good career choice.

We ask that you take this information with a grain of salt. Choosing a career based on how "hot" it will be in the future is like choosing a husband or wife based on life expectancy. Just because your mate's probably going to be around fifty years from now doesn't mean you're going to enjoy living with that person! Likewise, if you choose a job based solely on its future potential, you're asking for trouble. If it's not something that interests you now, it probably won't be something that interests you twenty years from now.

FASTEST GROWING INDUSTRIES

The *Career Guide to Industries*, published by the United States Bureau of Labor Statistics (yes, there's a bureau for labor statistics—your tax dollars hard at work), ranks careers from an industry perspective. The following industries are projected to grow faster than average between in the next decade.

Industry	Projected Rate of Growth
Computer and data processing services	95.7
Social services	93.1
Child care	73.0
Management and public relations	69.5
Motion picture production and distribution	60.8
Personnel supply services	56.6
Health services	43.4
Agriculture	40.5
Hotel and lodging	40.5
Amusement and recreation services	39.1
Air transportation	32.7
Eating and drinking places	33.0
Securities and commodities	29.9
Educational services	28.4
Advertising	27.5

SLOWEST GROWING INDUSTRIES

The Bureau of Labor Statistics' *Career Guide to Industries* also ranks the industries with the slowest projected growth rates. The following industries are projected to grow more slowly than average or decline in the next decade.

Industry	Projected Rate of Growth
Department stores	12.2
Public utilities	12.2
Radio and TV broadcasting	10.5
Banking	4.3
Aerospace manufacturing	2.5
Food processing	-0.4
Chemicals manufacturing (not drugs)	-4.0
Federal government	-5.2
Motor vehicle equipment manufacturing	-6.1
Mining and quarrying	-6.8
Steel manufacturing	-10.5
Oil and gas extraction	-14.3
Textile mill products manufacturing	-15.0
Electronics manufacturing	-16.3
Telephone communications	-20.6
Apparel manufacturing	-24.4

FASTEST GROWING OCCUPATIONS

The busy little beavers at the Bureau of Labor Statistics also put out a list of the fastest growing careers from an *employee's* perspective. The following careers are projected to grow the most quickly in the next decade.

Career	Projected Rate of Growth
Home health aide	138%
Human service worker	136%
Personal/home care aide	130%
Computer engineer/scientist	112%
Systems analyst	110%
Physical/corrective therapy assistant/aide	93%
Physical therapist	88%
Paralegal	86%
Special education teacher	74%
Medical assistant	71%
Private detective	70%
Correction officer	70%
Child care worker	66%
Travel agent	66%
Radiologic technologist/technician	63%
Nursery worker	62%
Medical records technician	61%
Operations research analyst	61%
Occupational therapist	60%
Legal secretary	57%
Kindergarten/preschool teacher	54%

Career	Projected Rate of Growth
Manicurist	54%
Producer/director/actor/entertainer	54%
Speech pathologist/audiologist	51%
Flight attendant	51%
Guard	51%
Insurance adjuster/examiner/investigator	49%
Respiratory therapist	48%

SECTION 2
FINDING A JOB

On Your Own

Freelancing and Consulting

If you're exploring the spectrum of career opportunities, don't overlook freelancing and consulting. Both jobs offer unparalleled freedom and flexibility. Of course, they're also financially risky and require the worker to supply his own benefits and insurance. Pros and cons aside, these career options do deserve further investigation.

What You Should Know About Freelancing

Full-time freelancing is an intriguing career option. Before you consider it seriously, though, we need to clear up some misconceptions about the job and give you an accurate picture of what it's like.

Contrary to popular belief, most freelancers do not always dress in sweats and a T-shirt, roll out of bed at noon, and take the day off whenever the urge to golf strikes them. Yes, there's freedom that comes with the job. Quite a bit of freedom, in fact. Some people have a hard time handling such freedom. They find it difficult to work with so many other options available to them. Before long, the line between freelancing and goofing off has been erased.

Freelancing requires a tremendous amount of discipline. If you don't have that kind of discipline, stick to the corporate world. Believe it or not, you'll probably be much happier in the long run.

As for the freelancer dress code . . . okay, that stereotype is true. With no clients to meet and no boss to impress, freelancers can (and usually do) wear their most casual attire to work. If you're a T-shirt-and-sweats kind of person, you may have what it takes to be a freelancer.

Regarding working hours, most freelancers spend as much time (if not more) slaving away in their offices as their counterparts in corporate America do. One of the few downsides of working for yourself at home is that you're never really off the clock. There's always something more that needs to be done, and, with your office so close, there's a constant feeling of needing to get back to work.

The true freedom that freelancers enjoy is the freedom to pursue and accept only the projects that interest them—or only the projects that are the most financially rewarding, depending on your mindset.

WHAT YOU SHOULD KNOW ABOUT CONSULTING

If you have an area of expertise—that is, a field in which you are more skilled or have more credentials or training than the general public—you have the potential to be a consultant (assuming, of course, that your area of expertise is of interest to other people).

Computer programmers, history professors, psychologists, and librarians have all served as consultants. Consulting opportunities aren't limited to careers, though. Collectors, hobbyists, and self-styled "experts" are often in demand as consultants.

The key to breaking into the consulting business is networking. Make a list of the people you know and the people your friends know. If you're serious about it, you'll probably end up with hundreds of names on your list, representing people from all walks of life. Identify at least five people who might be interested in your consulting services and contact them. From there, get in touch with church groups, clubs, senior centers, or fraternal organizations to see if they might have need for your expertise (whatever it may be).

After you get your first client or two, word of mouth will begin to spread. If you'd prefer to speed up that process, you might advertise your services in the Yellow Pages or in a local business paper. Direct mail and other promotional materials are also possibilities. If you're so inclined, you might even set up a web site to promote your consulting business.

Remind yourself, though, that in order to be taken seriously as a consultant, you must take yourself seriously. Present a professional appearance in everything you do. You should dress appropriately while you are on the job. You should carry yourself in a professional manner. Your business cards and stationery should also reflect your professionalism.

Depending on the job, you may charge clients by the hour, by the day, or on a per-project basis. If you're asked to give an estimate for your services, figure up the number of hours you anticipate spending on the project (padding your estimate with some extra hours in case of unforeseen delays) and then multiply that number by your hourly rate. The willingness of customers to pay your price will tell you whether you're charging too much.

FINAL ADVICE

A final word of advice to all would-be freelancers and consultants: Never dismiss a job offer without exploring it fully first. Sometimes the projects that seem like duds turn out to be the most profitable, both in exposure and in compensation.

It's Not Tax-Free Money

DON'T FORGET

Some new consultants and freelancers grow excited about their new income. The money often comes in a big check and **NO TAXES ARE WITHHELD!** Unfortunately, that doesn't mean that no taxes are due. A good investment of your time will be to visit a tax accountant who can explain what you need to do to avoid trouble with the IRS.

GOING MOBILE

SHOULD YOU RELOCATE FOR A JOB?

Imagine that you've been called back for a second interview with a company. They like you! They really like you! You're already imagining your name on the door of your office when the interviewer throws this question at you: "Would you be willing to relocate?"

Huh?

What would you say? We're talking about leaving friends and family members behind, for crying out loud! Would you actually consider packing up everything and moving to another city if it meant landing a sweet job?

To those of you who answered, "Sure, I'd consider relocating for the right position": *mazel tov.* You have answered wisely, my child.

To those of you who answered, "No way, bubba; I'm staying right where I'm at": wake up and smell the smoke. You've got a major career opportunity going up in flames.

KEEP AN OPEN MIND

The success of your job search may depend on your flexibility and mobility. One of the first things many interviewers and recruiters do when they talk to job candidates is determine their willingness to move. Because of today's worker-friendly market, executives and established employees don't feel as compelled to accept relocation assignments as they did in the past. That leaves positions to be filled by new hires.

Job candidates who absolutely refuse to consider relocating leave themselves with limited options. Candidates who keep an open mind about moving are likely to find jobs quicker, earn higher salaries, and discover greater career potential because of the many possibilities they leave available to themselves.

Wanna hear a cool little secret about job placement? *Being open* to moving to a new city for a job doesn't necessarily mean you'll have to *move* to a new city to get a job. Confused? Maybe an illustration will help.

Let's say Andy, who lives in Indianapolis, is offered an interview for a position in Chicago. "I hate traffic," he concludes, "so I don't think I'd last very long in Chi-town. Besides, everyone I know lives here." So Andy declines the interview.

Meanwhile, Louis, who also lives in Indy, is offered an interview for the same Chicago position. Though most of Louis' friends and family also live in Indianapolis, he decides to keep an open mind about relocating and goes to the interview. The hiring manager, impressed with Louis' résumé and presentation of himself, says, "We've got a small branch office in Carmel, just outside of Indianapolis, looking for an assistant account executive. Would you be interested?"

If you listen closely, you can hear Andy kicking himself.

Who's to say what might happen in an interview? Once the dialogue begins, you'd be surprised at how much can change. The point is, you shouldn't dismiss a job lead or interview because of location. The more doors you close in your job search, the tougher it's going to be.

QUESTION EVERYTHING

Let's say you keep an open mind about relocating. One day it happens—the call you thought would never come, the words you thought you'd never hear: "We'd like to make you an offer to become an assistant sales director . . . in Springfield."

The salary's right and the benefits are good. The only problem is that Springfield is over 500 miles away. You've got some serious considering to do and some hard questions to ask yourself.

How adventurous are you?

In order to make the move a positive experience, you'll need a sense of daring, a "pioneer" spirit. Are you up for change in your life? Can you get excited about living in a new city, with new friends and new opportunities? Relocation can open the door for tremendous growth, both professionally and personally.

What's your family going to say?

Are you married? Do you have kids? Do you have elderly parents who live near you? If you answered yes to any of these questions, your decision about moving becomes even trickier. If your spouse works, you'll need to consider his or her career prospects in your new city. If your kids are in school, you'll need to think about how disruptive a move would be for them. If your parents depend on you for transportation and care, you'll need to take their well-being into consideration.

What's in it for you?

What's the company offering you in exchange for your willingness to relocate? What's being done to ease the burden of moving? What expenses will be covered? Is the salary you're being offered satisfactory when you factor in the cost of living in your new city?

It's been said that aside from the death of a loved one or a serious illness, moving is the most traumatic experience in life. On the other hand, relocation has been the first step in many long, fulfilling careers. Either way, it's not a decision to be taken lightly.

HOW TO DECIDE WHETHER
A RELOCATION OFFER IS IN YOUR BEST INTEREST

How open to moving should you be in your job search? Before making any decisions, review these points.

1. Examine your career goals.

Take an honest look at where you are now in your career. Then think about where you'd like to be. Now ask yourself, "How will relocating help me get from Point A to Point B?" Think about where you need to be in order to maximize your career potential.

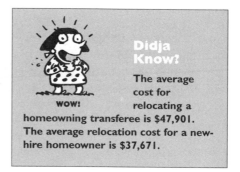

Didja Know?

The average cost for relocating a homeowning transferee is $47,901. The average relocation cost for a new-hire homeowner is $37,671.

2. Get your family's input.

Don't try to shoulder the responsibility for the decision all alone.
Seek the input of your spouse, children, parents, and siblings, if possible. Sure, they may have some strong opinions on the subject and may try to talk you out of moving, but they may also help you think of things you hadn't previously considered.

3. Talk to some job recruiters.

Recruiters have their fingers on the pulse of industry trends. They have information that may help you in your decision. For one thing, they can tell you how competitive an offer is and whether it's worth your while to pursue. They can also keep you informed of job possibilities closer to home.

4. Thoroughly interrogate your potential employer.

No question is a stupid question if it has to do with your future (not to mention the future of your family). When you talk to your family and to job recruiters, ask them to help you compile a list of important questions. Then put those questions to your future employer. Don't make a decision until you're satisfied with the answers you receive.

YOUR LIFE, IN A NUTSHELL

HOW TO CREATE AN EFFECTIVE RÉSUMÉ

Writing an effective résumé is one of the most difficult parts of a job search. It's also one of the most important. The résumé is the key that unlocks the door to your future employer. Once you're inside the door, you can impress people's socks off. But without a résumé, you won't get the opportunity. Here's what you need to do to create a door-opening résumé.

Step One: Write a mini-autobiography.

The first draft of your résumé should look like notes from a bragging seminar. Write down every job you've ever held, every award you've ever won, every citation you've ever earned, every hobby you've ever pursued.

You say you're naturally modest and have a hard time tooting your own horn? Get over it. When you work on your résumé, you're *allowed* to brag—you're *expected* to brag. What's more, you're probably not going to land the job you want *unless* you brag. So go ahead and write down all the wonderfully impressive things about yourself. No one's going to think you're conceited.

You say you're not sure how far back you should go in listing jobs and accomplishments? For now, go back as far as your memory takes you. Since this is a first draft, write down literally everything you can think of. Part-time jobs, school activities, sports participation, travel experiences, musical talent, foreign language fluency, computer skills, and charitable activities are all potential résumé material. Fill up several pages with your accomplishments and history.

Step Two: Secure inside information.
This is important: You'll need to find the job description of the position you're applying for. How? This book has a list of occupations and gives basic information you'll need for many jobs. Also, your library should have a copy of *The Dictionary of Occupational Titles.* This invaluable resource, which is used by the human resource departments of many major corporations in establishing job descriptions, should have exactly the information you're looking for. Look up the title of the job you're seeking and copy (that is, quote verbatim) *all* of the relevant material. Make sure you write down *exact* phrases. (We'll explain the importance of this task in Step Four.)

Step Three: Start weeding.
With the job description in front of you, go back through the "mini-autobiography" you wrote earlier and highlight all of the jobs, skills, and experiences that are even remotely related to the position you're seeking. Cross out everything else, regardless of how impressive it is. If it doesn't have some thing to do with the job you're seeking, save it for your real autobiography. The material you're left with will be the raw data from which you create your résumé.

Step Four: Spruce up your job history.
Starting with your current job and working backward in time, list the positions you've held that are related to the job you're seeking. Include the name and location of the employer, the number of years you worked there, and the title you held.

This is important: Under each position, list your responsibilities in that job. As you do this, though, take a look at the job description you copied earlier. Whenever possible, use phrases and sentences from the job description in detailing your previous responsibilities. It's an effective little trick in getting your résumé noticed. If the hiring manager sees the same phrases on your résumé that are on the job description, she'll likely view you as an obvious match for the position.

In addition to your responsibilities, you should also list your accomplishments in each position. Did you exceed your sales quota by 50 percent? Did you save the company $10,000 by suggesting a new way of doing things? Did you generate new business by going above and beyond the call of duty? If so, how? Write it down, and wherever possible, include numbers or percentages.

Step Five: Profile yourself.

Make room in your résumé for a four- or five-sentence overview of your qualifications. This is where you'll include personal traits and skills that didn't quite fit in your job descriptions. It's also where you'll catch the eye of the reader. Keep in mind that your goal is to grab the reader's attention and hold it. After that, you can wow him with your experience.

Step Six: Turn your words into literature.

It's time to move from outlines to paragraphs. Flesh out sentence fragments. Combine related items. Restructure copy so that it's interesting to read. Use verbs at the beginning of sentences to add punch. Polish the material, tweaking words here and there, to give it a rhythm.

If you find it difficult to bring life to your résumé, ask someone who's good with words to go over it and suggest changes or rewrite it. (As long as the experiences are yours, it doesn't really matter whose words are on your résumé.)

Step Seven: Select a look.

Next you need to choose a format for your résumé—that is, decide how you want it to look on the page. You may be tempted to use a fancy font as an attention getter. Don't. Instead, choose a font that is highly readable. You want your words to jump off the page. You don't want people to have to look closely at what you've written because most of them won't. Illegible résumés usually find their way to the circular file.

Once you've chosen a font, you'll need to spend some time working on a layout. How do you want to position the information on the page? What can you do to make the material inviting to a reader? Trial and error is usually the best method. Print out several different layout possibilities and decide which one works best. You might even poll a few other people to get their opinions.

Finding the right format for your résumé requires you to walk a fine line. On the one hand, you want your résumé to stand out in a crowd. On the other hand, you don't want to do anything too cutesy or radical. "Inconspicuously obvious" is what you're shooting for.

Step Eight: Give it a once-over, and then a twice-over, and then . . .
Even after you've written everything you want to say and formatted it to your satisfaction, your résumé still isn't finished. Proofreading is the final step—or steps—because you'll need to do it more than once.

Résumés are graded on a pass/fail basis. Quite simply, if there's one mistake on your résumé, it's a failure. If that sounds like pressure, it is. You need to read and reread your résumé until you're absolutely positive that it's flawless. If you don't trust your own editorial eye, ask others to read it over as well.

A résumé isn't something you want to knock off in one night. As we've tried to demonstrate with this list, there's quite a bit of work involved in crafting an effective résumé. But remember, your résumé is the first impression your potential employer will have of you. Make it a good one because you may not get a second chance.

RÉSUMÉ Q AND A

A one-page résumé seems kind of skimpy, like I haven't got much to say about myself. On the other hand, who's going to read two pages? How many pages should my résumé be?

There is no certain set length for résumés, though it's generally agreed that they shouldn't run shorter than a full page nor longer than two pages. Perhaps the best thing to do is to put yourself in the hiring manager's position. If you were that person, how excited would you be to read the second page of your résumé? Is it full of information that applies to the job you're seeking? Or is it repetitive, padded, and stretched uncomfortably to two pages? Let's put it this way: if you're scrambling for things to write after a page and a half, you should condense the information to one page. There's nothing skimpy about a well-prepared one-page résumé. On the other hand, if you can fill two pages with relevant information, you should do it.

The Bible and Your Career Decision

God cares about your decisions.

THE BIBLE SAYS

The Bible says:
"Trust the LORD with all your heart, and do not rely on your own understanding. In all your ways acknowledge him, and he will make your paths smooth. (Proverbs 3:5-6, God's Word).

Some people have said that I should "customize" my résumé, meaning that I should create a separate résumé for each company I apply to. That seems like a lot of work to me. Is it really necessary?

Yes and yes. Yes, it's a lot of work, and, yes, it's necessary. Remember, with your résumé, you're trying to match your experience as closely as possible to the company's job description. If the job descriptions of two different companies are slightly different, it would be worth your while to craft two slightly different résumés. That's not to say that you'll need to completely rewrite your résumé; usually, it's just a matter of emphasizing and rewording a couple of points.

What's the most important thing to remember concerning résumés?

Don't lie. The Bible says, "You may be sure that your sin will find you out" (Numbers 32:23). That's a good verse to keep in mind while you work on your résumé. Chances are, you're going to be tempted to stretch the truth a bit in order to position yourself as an ideal candidate for a job. Don't do it. If you lie (or even exaggerate) on your résumé, it's going to come back to haunt you. Your sin will be found out, and you will be humiliated. So save yourself the embarrassment and guilt, and just tell the truth.

SAMPLE RÉSUMÉ

Many word processors will help you write a résumé with an attractive template. The résumé on the next page was created with Microsoft Word.

BE SURE TO INCLUDE:

An objective. What can you contribute to the company? What would you like? Go beyond saying: "Get a job." This is a powerful line to many people who may read your résumé.

Education. If you graduated with a 4.0, say so. If you're GPA is not much to be proud of, don't include it. You should include your college and your degree. If you're fresh out of college it's acceptable to include your high school. Please, save your Jr. high GPA for the your own scrapbook.

Work history. Tell about your past experience. Make what you did sound as important and interesting as it really was. If you're just entering the full-time work force, you may not have much to include, but find something. Don't just list the obvious (For example, if you scooped ice cream at 31 Flavors, you probably developed skills in marketing and customer service.)

Other information. This is the chance to list items about yourself that make you extra attractive to the job.

Your address and phone. No duh, right? You'd be shocked at what some people (who don't get jobs) forget.

EVELYN JELICOL

Objective

To help promote Heavenly Pizza's products and gain an entry level position in marketing.

Education

1995–1998   Messiah College   Grantham, PA
- B.A., Business Administration and Marketing.   GPA 3.5.

Experience

1998-1999   AF&F Phone Company   Philadelphia, PA
Marketing Internship
- Wrote first draft of letters for mass mailings.
- Developed plan for an anti-slamming advertising campaign.
- Worked in phone bank making telemarketing calls.
- Worked on task force that created the successful marketing campaign: "Call your mother. It's only a dime."

1997   The College Reader   Grantham, PA
Advertising Editor
- Called area businesses to secure advertising.
- Creating page layouts for full page advertisements.
- Increased revenue for paper by thirty-five percent.
- Increaseddistribution fifteen percent.

Other information
- Skilled in the following software programs: Microsoft Word, Excel, Quark Xpress, and PageMaker.

PHONE (123) 098-7654 • E-MAIL ME@ISP.COM
12345 GRACE STREET • FAIR LAWN, NJ 12345

JUST LIKE A FIRST DATE

HOW TO PREPARE FOR A JOB INTERVIEW

Imagine that for one glorious night you're going on a date with the person of your dreams. Maybe it's a supermodel, maybe it's a rock star, maybe it's a Hollywood celebrity. Strangely enough, the only thing you really know about your date is that the person is looking for a relationship. You also happen to know that you possess some of the qualities and characteristics the person is looking for in a significant other. (Don't ask how you know all this; just buy into the premise.)

Unfortunately, your date has no idea who you are or what you're like. You have one night to showcase your best qualities, to convince this person that you, above the thousands and thousands of others vying for your date's affections, are the perfect candidate for a relationship. How much time do you think you'd put into making sure that everything went right that night? What kind of planning would you do?

The same questions might be asked of the interviewing process. In an interview, you have one chance to impress an organization that has no idea who are. You have one opportunity to prove to the company that you're the perfect candidate for a long-term employment relationship. How much time will you spend planning for that opportunity? Here are some things you might want to consider doing.

DETECTIVE WORK

As a rule, the more you know about the company you're interviewing with, the better your interview will go. That's where research comes in. You'll need to gather as much information as you can about the organization. Most employers will be impressed that you're interested enough in their corporation to research it before you interview.

The first place you should go as a researcher is to your networking contacts. Find out what they know about the company and what their opinions are of it. Next pore over trade journals, newspapers, and business directories to find information on things like how long the company has been in business, what kind of products or services it offers, and how profitable it is. Extra bonus points for finding information on the company's biggest success and its most glaring failure.

RÉSUMÉ REVIEW

The first commandment of job interviewing is "Know thy résumé." Not only do you want to be able to answer any questions employers may have about it, you also want to be able to relate the skills described on it to other questions the interviewer asks. To do that, you'll need to know your résumé forward, backward, and inside out. By the time you get to the interview, your résumé should be as familiar to you as your favorite Bible verse or the lyrics of your favorite song.

DETAIL COVERAGE

Plan and prepare yourself for *every* aspect of the interview. Don't risk wearing the wrong clothes. Some time before the interview, drive to the company during business hours and simply observe the workers coming and going. Not only will this give you an idea of how to dress for your interview, it will also acquaint you with the best route to the office. You don't want to take a chance on being late to the interview because you got lost on the way! Likewise, find an open parking area near the company so that you're not sweating finding a parking space before the interview. Plan to arrive at the office fifteen minutes before your interview. Allow plenty of time to get there.

Remember, the more you plan and prepare for your big "date," the better chance you'll have of catching that certain someone's eye and sparking an interest in a long-term relationship.

WHAT TO EXPECT AFTER THE HANDSHAKE

TEN COMMON INTERVIEW QUESTIONS-AND HOW TO ANSWER THEM

You may be surprised to learn how predictable job interviews are. Sure, each interviewer brings uniqueness and individuality to the proceedings, but the questions themselves tend to fall into the same few categories. We've listed ten sample questions below. And while we don't guarantee that all ten will be asked in every interview, we will say this: if you're fully prepared to answer these questions when you walk into an interview, you have no reason to be concerned.

1. Tell me about yourself.

Don't be fooled by the casual tone of this common icebreaker. This is not preinterview chit-chat. The last thing you want to do is toss off a casual answer. ("Oh, there's really not much to tell. I'm single. I just moved to Atlanta, and I figured it was time to start looking for a job.")

A job interview is all about selling yourself, and this request is an open invitation to begin your sales pitch. As harmless as the statement sounds, this is probably the most critical point of the interview. The first impression you make will affect the rest of the interview.

It's extremely likely that this request will pop up somewhere in the interview, so prepare for it. Use this opportunity to portray yourself, not only as a valuable addition to the company, but also as a person others would like to get to know—and work with.

2. What interests you about this position?

If you did your prep work, gathering information about the company and researching the job description, now's the time to put that information to use.

"My goal is to put my sales skills to use for a rising business with the potential to become a leader in the industry. For the past 4 years, this company has maintained an annual growth rate of at least 8 percent, so I think it fits the description of a "rising" company. As a sales associate at Jones' Collectibles, I brought in over $50,000 in orders, 30 percent of that in

WOW!

Ten Things You Should Never Say at a Job Interview

1. "I know my rights—I'm not answering any questions until I talk to my lawyer."
2. "My salary history is none of your business, Tubby."
3. "Overtime would be a problem because my mom doesn't like it when I'm out after dark."
4. "Uh oh, I'm hearing the voices again."
5. "I'd have to say *The Jerry Springer Show* has been the biggest influence in my life."
6. "Do I get paid for this interview?"
7. "To tell you the truth, I'm only here because all my other options fell through."
8. "Can I get some coffee? I was up playing Nintendo all night, and I am wasted!"
9. "I wouldn't pay too much attention to that résumé if I were you—I made most of that stuff up."
10. "Are we almost done? This is getting pretty boring."

repeat business. I believe that my experience in closing deals and building long-term customer relationships will serve me well as an assistant sales manager here."

The more you know about the company you're interviewing with and the position you're interviewing for, the more brownie points you'll score with your interviewer. At the same time, though, always remember to use that information in conjunction with your own abilities and experience.

3. What is your greatest strength and your biggest weakness?

This is another question you can prepare for. Before the interview, take a look at the description of the job you're interviewing for. The characteristic that stands out most in that description will be your greatest strength when this question arises. For example, if the description uses the phrase "self-starter," suddenly your greatest strength is your ability to motivate yourself.

This is important: We are *not* advocating lying. If you can't put two sentences together, don't claim the ability to express yourself as your greatest strength—even if it is in the job description. We're advising you to find a strength that *does* apply to you and focus on it.

As for the weakness part of the question, be careful. The last thing you want to do is go confessional and share some deep dark character flaw. ("When I'm caught in a lie, I often resort to violence.") Think of a weakness that would not affect your ability to do the job you're interviewing for. Then follow up your answer with a list of actions you've taken to improve in your area of weakness.

4. Do you prefer to work alone or as part of a team?

The key here is to emphasize your flexibility. As a "self-starter," you're certainly capable of handling and completing assignments on your own, without having to be told what to do or when to do it. However, as a "team player" (remember, everyone loves a team player), you also recognize and welcome the contributions that others can bring to a project. (Be ready with some examples of assignments you've completed on your own and those on which you've worked with others.)

There's an unspoken aspect of this question that you should be aware of. In determining how well you work in groups, the interviewer is also trying to find out whether you're more comfortable in the role of leader or follower. *Here's a tip:* Don't portray yourself as a follower. You may be a reluctant leader, but the interviewer needs to know that you have the ability to take charge of a situation when necessary.

5. How well do you work under pressure?

This is a logical question since most jobs come with a fair amount of stress. In answering it, though, don't portray yourself as someone who eats stress for breakfast. In fact, don't portray yourself as anything other than human. You can talk about how stress helps you achieve a laser-sharp focus on the task at hand or how it can galvanize a team of workers and bring them closer together. But you'll also need to talk about what you do at home and in your spare time to relieve stress. Nobody wants to hire a heart attack waiting to happen.

It (almost) goes without saying that this question begs for an example of how you handled a

Two Tips to a Good First Impression

CATCH A CLUE   *I. Arrive to a job interview early.* This will give you a chance to catch your breath, calm your nerves, comb your hair, and warm your hands before that first handshake.

2. Dress conservatively. Your outfit is not the place to make a statement about yourself. For most business situations, a conservative suit is best for the interview. You should dress well even if the company, or division, for which you are interviewing is fairly casual.

stressful situation in the past. Be sure to emphasize the problem-solving and decision-making skills you honed in your previous employment.

6. Where do you see yourself five years from now?

This a loaded question, one that's very difficult to answer. On the one hand, you want the interviewer to know that you have long-term goals. On the other hand, you don't want to seem overly ambitious or, even worse, naive. Perhaps your safest route is to talk about the importance of continuing education to you. After all, the more you prepare yourself with education, the better able you'll be to recognize and successfully pursue new career opportunities.

7. What do you like to do in your spare time?

This is a broad question, to be sure. As you think about your answer, keep this in mind: you can't go wrong with team sports and volunteer work. Participation in sports indicates your willingness and ability to work with others as a team, an important trait in most jobs. Volunteer work indicates that you have a concern for others and the motivation and drive to act on that concern.

A popular offshoot of the "spare time" question is to ask what was the last book you read and what was the last movie you saw. If you're really into interview preparation, read a book or see a movie that deals with handling pressure, overcoming obstacles, or working as a team. You can then emphasize the importance of those traits in your own life when you talk about the movies you've seen or the books you've read.

8. Describe a time when you succeeded at something. Describe a time when you failed at something. Which experience was more valuable to you?

Your success story should be directly related to some aspect of the job you're interviewing for. For example, you might talk about how, in your previous position, you succeeded in increasing product output by 25 percent by streamlining the production process.

In talking about failure, your goal is to portray yourself as someone who's experienced enough failure not to be scared of it—but *not* as someone who is prone to failure. Be ready to talk about the steps you've taken to correct past failures and what you've learned from those failures.

9. According to your résumé, you were with your previous company only six months before you left. Can you explain why?

"Danger, Captain! The Résumé is under attack! The outer hull has been breached, and I don't know how much more she can take!"

If you've got a time gap—like, say, you were out of work for a year—or some other flaw in your résumé: some recruiter or interviewer is bound to notice and ask you about it. You must be prepared with an honest (but not overly revealing) answer. If you're not, your résumé will cast doubts on your reliability and truthfulness.

10. What do you have to offer this company?

You may also encounter the more blunt version of this question: "Why should we hire you over the other candidates for the job?" To answer it, you'll need to identify something unique in yourself, something you bring to the table that no one else can offer. This question calls for blatant self-promotion. If you're uncomfortable with that, you may need to practice touting yourself before the interview.

These questions should give you a place to start in preparing for job interviews. When you feel comfortable in your ability to answer these ten questions, you'll be ready to hit the interview circuit.

THE ART OF THE SCHMOOZE

NETWORKING

Pssst-hey, you. Yeah, you with the book. You look like you could use a business tip. It's practically guaranteed to speed up any job search. You interested? Yeah, I thought you might be. Okay, lean in close. I don't want to give this tip away to everyone. Here it is: When it comes to business, often it's not *what* you know, it's *who* you know.

You read that right. You could be the most qualified person in the world for a job and never even get your foot in the company door. Meanwhile, some bozo with half your experience waltzes in, aces what should have been *your* interview, gets *your* job, and starts collecting *your* paychecks! Why? Because he knew the right person.

Kind of makes you want to spit, doesn't it? Well, the way I see it, you've got two choices. You can either stand around and complain about how unfair the system is or you can start playing the networking game.

Networking is a fancy name for making contact with people who may be able to help you with your career. If you're a "people person," naturally outgoing and gregarious, networking will probably be enjoyable for you. On the other hand, if you're shy and introverted by nature, the thought of "schmoozing" probably gives you sweaty palms.

The good news is that networking is a skill anyone can learn. Here are some helpful hints to get you started.

DON'T STRAY TOO FAR FROM YOUR COMFORT ZONE

You're not going to become a world-class schmoozer overnight, so don't try to. Start out slowly. Your best bet is to begin with a family friend or a member of your church, someone a little less threatening than a total stranger would be. Practice your information-gathering techniques on him. Talk about the career you're pursuing and seek advice. Ask the person if he has any contacts in your chosen field (or even in a related field) or other people with whom you can discuss your career.

From there, you can expand your networking circle. After you've exhausted your supply of nonthreatening contacts, you can begin talking to people you don't know. Ideally, by this time, you'll have enough networking practice to make it a comfortable situation for you.

GIVE OTHER PEOPLE A CHANCE

Don't assume that everyone you meet is an introvert who would prefer to be left alone. Believe it or not, there are many people in this world who would take a genuine interest in your career search. Most of your contacts will probably be flattered by the fact that you're seeking their opinion. Don't forget, ego is a powerful motivator. You may be surprised at the lengths to which some of your contacts will go to help you.

That's not to say you won't encounter some people who are too busy to help you and some who are just plain rude. When you do, shrug it off and move on to the next contact. You'll find that these people are a definite minority.

FIND MOTIVATION WHERE YOU CAN

Networking is a tough job and an easy one to put off. But the more you delay it, the longer and more frustrating your job search will become. What you need is proper motivation, a kick in the seat of the pants to get you started. Allow us to provide the shoe.

Remember that bozo in the introduction who got the job that should have gone to you? There's another one out there just like him. And right now, he's making a list of people he can call to help him with his job search. He's setting up meetings with them to "pick their brains" about the business world and "get their advice" on his career search. And he's practicing his schmoozing techniques, hoping that they will land him a job. But not just any job—a job that should have gone to you.

You can't allow another bozo to land a job that should have gone to you. Face your fears, take a deep breath, pick up the phone, and call someone you (or your parents) know who can help you with your job search.

DON'T DO ANYTHING STUPID

Because every networking opportunity is a unique event, it would be foolish to say that there is one specific method for dealing with a contact. There are, however, some principles you must keep in mind while you're networking. Don't ever make the person feel as if he is being "used." Treat him as a valued advisor, not a resource.

Don't waste the person's time. Be prepared with a short agenda. Don't be a pest, firing question after question until the person gets sick of you. Make sure you follow through when you're given the name of a potential contact. If someone takes the time to help you in your career search, it would be extremely rude to blow off that help.

Always say thank you. Send a card or make a phone call to let the person know you appreciate his help.

THE QUEST FOR A HIGHER TAX BRACKET

HOW TO ASK FOR A RAISE

In a perfect world, you wouldn't have to ask for a raise. Your boss, recognizing your value to the company and realizing how grossly underpaid you are, would simply walk in one day and announce that he's doubling your salary. Those of you living in such a perfect world need not read any further.

The rest of you, however, are probably tired of waiting for your boss to make the first move. It's time for you to take matters into your own hands. But remember, there's a right way and a wrong way to approach your supervisor about a raise. Here are some dos and don'ts you might want to think about before you go barging into your boss's office.

Do be prepared with a list of reasons why you deserve a raise.
Make a list of your accomplishments and your contributions to the corporation. If you've recently brought in a large account, include that on your list. If you found a way to save the company a significant amount of money, write that down. If you've improved quality of service in a measurable way or launched a new product line, mention that. You might also list an outstanding performance review, an increase in your department's productivity, an earned credential, or your mastery of a new job-related skill.

All of these are compelling reasons for a raise, arguments with the potential to convince even the stingiest manager. Most importantly, they highlight your individual contributions to the company.

Don't expect your boss to be swayed by your reasons.

Unless your list of reasons includes actions that are truly above and beyond the call of duty, your boss may counter that you've simply been fulfilling your job description. She may point out that other employees have contributed just as much, if not more, to the department as you have.

Put simply, your boss may be a better negotiator than you are. Don't expect her to cave in to your request for a raise, even if you have what you think are some pretty convincing reasons.

Do time your request carefully.

The timing of your request is perhaps the most important factor in determining whether or not you get your raise. For example, it's always best to ask for a raise during a tight job market. Sometimes companies can't afford to lose good employees to higher-paying competitors. Considering the money and resources (not to mention the time) it would take to find a replacement for you, it would probably make better financial sense for your company to simply give you your raise.

You also want to time your request so that it coincides with an outstanding achievement on your part. It's hard to turn down someone for a raise after you've just praised his work. Another good time to pop the question is when another company is courting you with promises of a salary increase. Use any leverage you can get to help your company recognize you're worth more money than you're being paid.

Don't request a raise if you're not in your boss's good graces.

Just because the guy in the next cubicle was given a raise doesn't mean that you're entitled to one, too. If your work is mediocre or unsatisfactory to your boss, don't put yourself (or her) in an awkward position by asking for a raise. You'll come off looking like a clueless buffoon.

Here's another tip: Don't ask for a raise when your company is facing layoffs. Sometimes the squeaky wheel gets the grease; other times, the squeaky wheel gets the pink slip. Know when to be thankful for what you have.

Do be prepared for rejection.

No matter how persuasive your argument is, there's a good chance you're going to hear, "I'm sorry, a raise is not part of your salary structure right now," or some other form of corporate doublespeak. The translation is the same: no extra cash for you! How will you react? How *should* you react?

The key is to be prepared for this possibility. How strongly do you feel about the raise? Is it something you're willing to leave the company over? Chances are, unless you have an offer from another company, giving notice won't be an option.

You *will* want to let your boss know that you're disappointed. Do it in a straightforward and humble way, though. Don't pout, whine, or talk about how unfair it is. Act like the professional you are. End the discussion by asking your boss when would be a good time to talk again about your raise.

Don't overreact to a rejection.

Don't let your emotions get the better of you. You'll end up saying things you'll regret later—things that may ruin your chances for a future raise. Don't take the rejection personally. Remind yourself that it's a business decision, not a reflection of your worth. Most importantly, though, don't make idle threats. Don't paint yourself into a corner. Don't say, "If I don't get this raise, I'm going to . . ." Chances are,

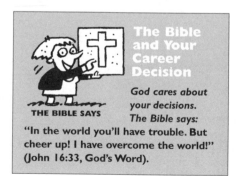

The Bible and Your Career Decision

THE BIBLE SAYS

God cares about your decisions. The Bible says: "In the world you'll have trouble. But cheer up! I have overcome the world!" (John 16:33, God's Word).

you'll end up crawling back to your boss offering embarrassed apologies.

HOW MUCH IS YOUR JOB REALLY WORTH?

A LOOK AT COMPENSATION AND BENEFITS

Pop quiz, hotshot: Company A offers you a starting salary of $48,000 a year. Company B (of "Boogie Woogie Bugle Boy" fame) offers you a salary of $51,000 a year. Which company is offering the better compensation package?

    (a) Company A
    (b) Company B
    (c) The answer cannot be determined based on this information.

You didn't choose "b," did you? Surely you're not the type who thinks only in terms of money. You've been around; you know that salary is only one small part of career compensation. And you know that if you were to base a career decision solely on the size of the paycheck, you might not get the best financial package available. You *do* know that, don't you?

There's More to Compensation Than Money

Experienced job hunters never talk about *salary;* they talk about a *compensation package.* It should be pointed out that there is no such thing as a "standard" compensation package. These packages vary not only from company to company, but from individual to individual. Some executives and other corporate VIPs are actively involved in designing their compensation packages. Most working stiffs, on the other hand, usually have no say in their compensation packages.

Why the need for compensation packages? Most companies are bound by rigid salary structures. Even if they wanted to increase a worker's pay by 10 percent, they couldn't, unless that raise was part of the worker's predetermined salary increase.

Such restrictions can pose problems when these companies are competing for a star job candidate. If the candidate were to demand a salary higher than the company's predetermined range for the position, the company would be forced to decline—and lose a potentially great worker in the process.

That's where compensation packages come in. Because they're not officially considered salary, compensation packages are not affected by the company's rigid pay structure.

In addition to salary, compensation packages may include the following:

Signing bonus—a large chunk of change the employee receives simply for committing to the company. In extreme cases, signing bonuses may be equal to or more than a year's salary.

Work-at-home privileges—an arrangement in which the employee is allowed to perform his duties from the comfort of his home office one or two days a week. In some cases, this arrangement includes equipping the employee's home office with the latest technology.

Education reimbursement—a guarantee to pay for any relevant training programs, seminars, or classes the employee chooses to attend.

Company car—something to make the commute to and from work a little more bearable.

Club membership—an opportunity to tone your body or improve your golf game at the company's expense.

Stock options—a perk with the potential to reap some serious cash, depending on the market.

BENEFITS TO LOOK FOR

While only a select few can demand a deluxe compensation package, most full-time company employees receive some kind of a benefits package. Here's a brief rundown of the benefits that are often provided by employers.

Health Plan
Though there are a variety of plans available, most of them cover the majority of employee medical expenses, minus standard deductibles. Psychiatric care, short-term disability, long-term disability, prescription drug programs, wellness programs, and preventative dental care are also part of most plans, though they usually carry with them certain stipulations and restrictions.

Paid Vacations
Usually vacation time is based on the amount of days you worked the previous calendar year. In a sense, you "earn" it. Some companies place restrictions on how much vacation time can be used in one stretch. Some companies pay employees for vacation time that is not used; others allow it to "roll over" into the next year, giving employees opportunities to store up boatloads of time off.

Paid Holidays
The recognized paid holidays for most companies are New Year's Day, Memorial Day, Independence Day, Labor Day, Thanksgiving, and Christmas. When these holidays fall on Saturday or Sunday, the time off usually comes on the preceding Friday or the following Monday. Additionally, many corporations designate one or two "floating holidays," usually around Thanksgiving and Christmas, to maximize seasonal time off.

Sick Leave

Most corporations offer a set number of paid sick days for their employees to use when they don't feel well enough to work. Unlike vacation days, when sick days aren't used, they usually are lost and do not "roll over" to the next year.

Personal Leave Days

In addition to paid vacations, holidays, and sick leave, many companies offer personal leave days to their employees. These are like "Get out of jail free" cards in Monopoly. They allow you to skip a day of work (after notifying management of your plans, of course) without having your pay docked. Usually the number of personal leave days you're entitled to depends on how long you've been with the company.

Retirement Benefits

Most companies offer retirement plans for their employees, funds set aside by the company that employees may collect after they retire.

Investment Plans

A growing number of corporations are providing 401K or IRA plans for their employees. Some companies even offer a "matching" program in which they will match the amount of money an employee invests in the program, up to a certain dollar amount.

Profit Sharing

Some corporations choose to give their employees a stake in the company's financial success, handing out bonuses after profitable periods.

Continuing Education

Many companies foot the bill for employees to attend professional seminars and continuing education classes.

Compensation and benefits packages are "hidden money." You must give them as much consideration as you give salary when you consider a job offer.

A LITTLE HELP

WHAT YOU SHOULD KNOW ABOUT RECRUITERS

Some people call them placement-firm representatives. Others refer to them as professional recruiters. But to most people, they're "headhunters," career-search professionals who get paid to match up job seekers with job openings.

Many job seekers like the idea of someone else looking out for their career welfare. Others find headhunters to be a nuisance, preferring the do-it-yourself approach to job hunting. For those of you who aren't sure how you feel about headhunters, we provide the following overview of the recruiting industry.

WHO'S WHO IN PLACEMENT FIRMS

If you've looked into using a headhunter or recruiter in your job search, you were probably confronted with a bewildering array of options. For the uninitiated, navigating the waters of the job-placement industry can be an intimidating experience. How are you supposed to know the difference between an executive marketing career firm and a contingency recruiting firm? More importantly, how are you supposed to know which one is better for you?

Here's a brief guide to help you distinguish among the different types of firms available to job seekers. While these thumbnail sketches may not clear up the job-placement picture entirely for you, they will help you sort out some of the players.

Retained executive-search firm

This organization specializes in finding upper-level candidates and works exclusively on retainer. This means the firm gets paid whether or not a candidate is hired. The traditional payment breakdown is one-third of the fee upfront, one-third after thirty days, and one-third at the end of the assignment.

Contingency recruiting firm

This agency concentrates on placing candidates in mid- to senior-level positions. Fees are paid on a contingency basis by companies who have hired the firm. A contingency arrangement means the firm doesn't get paid until it finds a candidate who is hired for the position. Contingency firms often specialize in certain industries or functions.

Employment or personnel agency

This company generally places staff employees in clerical, skilled, or semi-skilled positions. Fees are paid on a contingency basis by employers who have hired the agency.

Applicant paid fee (APF) agency

This firm focuses solely on unskilled laborers, such as drivers, cooks, custodians, and machinists.

Temporary or interim staffing firm

This agency supplies staff for temporary projects or contract positions. However, the lines between temporary staffing firms and full-time firms are beginning to blur. Often companies use temporary staffers on a "trial basis" before offering them full-time positions.

Outplacement firm

This organization is paid by client companies to offer career guidance and job-search assistance to employees who have been laid off or dismissed. Résumé preparation, job-search training, counseling, secretarial assistance, and office support are just some of the services offered by an outplacement firm.

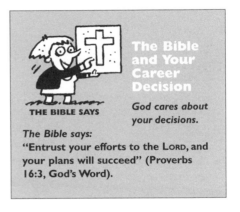

The Bible and Your Career Decision

THE BIBLE SAYS *God cares about your decisions.*

The Bible says:
"Entrust your efforts to the Lord, and your plans will succeed" (Proverbs 16:3, God's Word).

Executive marketing career firm

BEWARE THIS ORGANIZATION! This firm charges job seekers significant upfront fees, promising extensive job-search assistance, from résumé preparation to notification of job openings.

Attention, Attention: Many executive marketing career firms have come under suspicion and drawn widespread criticism lately for aggressive sales tactics, inadequate service, and outrageous fees. We recommend that you avoid contact with these firms.

WHAT YOU SHOULD KNOW ABOUT HEADHUNTERS

If you decide to use a recruiter in your job search, you'll need to do some research to find out which agencies are right for you. As we mentioned in the profile, certain recruiters specialize by industry and function. They work exclusively with a narrow range of job seekers. If your background does not match the requirements they're looking for, they will not consider you. To avoid wasting everyone's time, check out a directory of recruiting firms or talk to a trade association representative to get the names of the agencies that are right for you.

THE BIBLE SAYS   *God cares about your decisions.*

The Bible says:
"**Whatever happens, give thanks, because it is God's will in Christ Jesus that you do this**" (I Thessalonians 5:18, God's Word).

Once you've found a firm that suits your needs, provide your recruiter with as much information as possible. Send a copy of your résumé and a brief cover letter that includes your salary requirements, your current employment status, the type of position you're seeking, and a brief summary of your qualifications.

Stay in contact with the recruiter, but do not become a pest. Send an occasional e-mail message to update your file or your employment status. Give the recruiter time and space to do his job.

Finally, don't panic if you don't get interviews right away. And for goodness' sake, don't take your frustration out on the recruiter. He's at the mercy of the job market every bit as much as you are. Don't forget, it's in the headhunter's best interest to place you in a job. When the right position becomes available, you'll be called.

As long as you avoid the career-marketing firms that charge upfront fees for their services, you really can't go wrong with a recruiting agency. It's a matter of preference. Do you want to enlist the services of professionals or would you prefer to conduct your job search on your own?

WHO MAKES WHAT?

A GUIDE TO SALARY AVERAGES

Salary chart? Why would you be interested in a salary chart? You know that money can't make you happy. You know that the "love of money is a root of all kinds of evil" (1 Timothy 6:10). You know that "you cannot serve both God and money" (Luke 16:13). You know the corrupting power of filthy lucre. You know that wealthy people are often the most unhappy. You know that—

What's that? You say you're just looking for a general idea of how much you can expect to make in your chosen field? You say that you have no strong attachments to money, that your primary goals are to honor the Lord, support your family, and find fulfillment in your work?

Oh.

In that case, here is a salary chart that includes a wide variety of careers. How does your chosen field compare with some of the others? Is the annual salary higher, lower, or pretty comparable to what you expected? (If you don't find the exact field you're looking for, you'll probably find a field close enough for comparison.)

Keep in mind as you look through the salaries, though, that these are very broad averages. Depending on where you live and how high the demand is for your skills, your salary may differ significantly from the figures we've listed here. (To put it in the jargon of automobile advertising, your mileage may vary.) Our goal was merely to give you a starting point for salary comparison.

Occupation   *Average Salary*

Occupation	Average Salary
Accountant	$43,200
Accounting clerk	$27,500
Adjustment clerk	$22,400
Administrative assistant	$32,750
Advertising account executive	$36,200
Advertising art director	$46,500
Advertising copywriter	$42,000
Advertising creative director	$75,700
Advertising media director	$42,100
Assembler	$23,350
Associate producer	$30,200
Auditor	$44,900
Benefits manager	$61,900
Bill collector	$22,400
Bookkeeper	$28,400
Building manager	$43,000
Chemical engineer	$63,000
Cinematographer	$28,100
Civil engineer	$49,500
Clerical supervisor	$31,000
Commercial artist	$33,100
Computer applications programmer	$42,350
Computer applications systems analyst	$51,900
Computer artist	$31,100
Computer database analyst	$58,100
Computer engineer	$54,900
Computer help desk manager	$48,900
Computer information services manager	$98,300
Computer operator	$27,500

Occupation	Average Salary
Computer program analyst	$52,200
Computer scientist	$48,600
Computer software engineer	$57,350
Controller	$79,900
Correction officer	$28,800
Credit/collection manager	$60,400
Customer service representative	$27,000
Data entry operator	$22,100
Dental hygienist	$42,400
Designer	$30,850
Dietitian	$40,000
Director	$63,850
Electrical engineer	$53,200
Employee relations manager	$54,300
Engineering manager	$65,700
Executive secretary	$31,200
File clerk	$15,000
Financial services sales representative	$59,600
Flight attendant	$36,450
Food service worker	$17,700
Gaffer	$36,900
Health care support specialist	$31,050
Heavy machine operator	$30,000
Home health aide	$16,300
Human resources information services manager	$62,900
Human resources general worker	$33,800
Human resources training manager	$59,900
Insurance adjuster	$38,200
Labor relations manager	$70,000

Occupation	*Average Salary*
Laboratory technologist	$31,300
Lawyer	$70,100
Legal secretary	$33,000
Light machine operator	$22,850
Loan officer	$37,400
Mailroom supervisor	$20,600
Maintenance supervisor	$39,600
Management analyst	$48,200
Management support specialist	$38,250
Manufacturing production scheduler	$34,700
Manufacturing production supervisor	$51,800
Marketing manager	$53,600
Mechanical engineer	$47,150
Medical secretary	$29,800
Musician	$30,900
Nuclear medicine technician	$42,100
Nurse aide	$17,500
Occupational therapist	$46,800
Office manager	$35,400
Packaging supervisor	$41,200
Paralegal	$32,000
Payroll supervisor	$43,000
Personal service worker	$17,200
Pharmacist	$47,400
Pharmacy technician	$23,900
Physical therapist	$51,550
Physical therapy assistant	$23,590
Physician	$96,600
Physician assistant	$40,400

Occupation	*Average Salary*
Producer	$49,000
Public relations representative	$32,000
Purchasing agent	$38,000
Quality assurance inspector	$52,000
Radiology technician	$38,000
Receptionist	$18,100
Recruiter	$42,000
Registered nurse	$42,000
Respiratory therapist	$37,400
Safety manager	$59,200
Sales clerk	$20,500
Scriptwriter	$34,500
Secondary school teacher	$36,800
Security officer	$19,700
Service manager	$48,300
Shipping/receiving clerk	$13,500
Social worker	$33,900
Special education teacher	$37,100
Speech/language pathologist	$42,700
Sports instructor/coach	$22,900
Teacher aide	$16,000
Ultrasound technician	$39,600
University faculty	$44,800
Video editor	$53,000
Videographer	$35,200
Vocational training instructor	$33,800
Webmaster	$65,700
Word processing operator	$20,500
Writer/editor	$38,900

THE ENDLESS PURSUIT OF KNOWLEDGE...
AND A BIGGER PAYCHECK

IS IT WORTH YOUR WHILE TO GET A MASTER'S DEGREE?

President Harry Truman never attended college. Neither did inventor George Eastman, author Ernest Hemingway, or oil magnate John D. Rockefeller.

ABC news anchor Peter Jennings never finished high school. Neither did auto manufacturer Henry Ford, former British prime minister John Major, or inventors Wilbur and Orville Wright.

Inventor Thomas Edison never made it past grade school. Neither did author Mark Twain, billionaire industrialist Andrew Carnegie, or labor leader Samuel Gompers.

It's safe to say that education and career success don't *always* go hand in hand. But is that true for your career plans?

Remember, as brilliant and successful as these famous men were (and are), none of them could have become a doctor. For some careers, advanced education is a necessity.

We're going to assume that most of you reading this book have earned (or will earn) a bachelor's degree. The choice facing you now is whether or not to pursue a master's degree. Let's take a look at the issue.

DO IT FOR THE RIGHT REASONS

If you're looking for a consensus among career "experts" on the subject of graduate schools, good luck. Opinions vary on the topic. Some people view a master's degree as a logical step in the natural progression from undergraduate studies to career. Others view it as an overrated tactic for increasing one's salary value.

Some people argue that a master's degree is necessary for anyone who hopes to reach the upper echelons of management one day. Others counter that a master's degree postpones a person's entry into the business world, taking up time that could be better spent in on-the-job training.

Not surprisingly, there are statistics to back up both points of view. (If you look hard enough, you can find statistics to back up just about anything.) An October 1997 report in *Phi Delta Kappan* claimed that *16* percent of the MBA graduates from Stanford University, which boasts one of the most prestigious programs in the nation, were unable to find jobs. As you might imagine, graduates of less-renowned MBA programs faced even steeper odds. Forty percent of the graduates from Ohio State's business school rolled snake eyes in their job search.

On the other hand, a *Los Angeles Times* article from January 9, 1998, reported that the average salary offered to University of California-Irvine MBA candidates is about $60,000, up 10 percent from the last survey. With bonuses and incentives, the starting salary is actually closer to $75,000

An MBA, or any master's degree, *may* increase your starting salary. On the other hand, it *may* just make you one of the most educated people in the unemployment line. *Bottom line:* A master's degree is not an automatic ticket to an executive lifestyle. If you're in grad school for the money, you may be disappointed.

Don't misunderstand, though. There are many excellent reasons for continuing your education beyond undergraduate studies. Obviously, chief among these reasons is a hunger for knowledge. If learning is your priority, if you're not simply delaying your entrance into the business world, and if you have the resources to afford it, graduate school may prove to be a fulfilling experience.

Another legitimate reason for graduate studies is the pursuit of a dream job. We mentioned earlier that some careers, such as the medical profession, require advanced studies. Other careers, such as investment banking or technology management are simply not feasible without (at least) a graduate degree.

THE HARD WAY MAY BE THE BEST WAY

Some people choose to delay graduate studies until later in their careers. In doing so, they create a scheduling nightmare for themselves. Imagine trying to juggle a job, a family, and grad school classes at the same time! Those who've done it often talk about their experiences in tones usually reserved for war veterans. They emerge battle scarred, weary, and shell-shocked.

Believe it or not, these people may have the right idea. Not that we're advocating insane schedules, mind you. Instead, we're suggesting that grad school may be most beneficial to those who have several years of on-the-job experience. These people know what they want to learn. They can take an active role in their education. And perhaps most importantly, they are able to apply what they learn immediately in a work setting.

By contrast, a young buck fresh out of college has only the vaguest notion of what will be profitable to him in grad school. More often than not, he will choose a course of study based on the recommendations of others and hope that the material is applicable to his future career.

The decision whether to attend graduate school or not is not one to be taken lightly. Unless your career choice demands it, you should not automatically assume that grad school is the next step after college.

THE LURE OF DO-IT-YOURSELF

WHY BECOME SELF-EMPLOYED?

Who, in his right mind, would ever want to work for himself? What would make a person turn his back on a steady paycheck and the security that comes with working for an established company or organization? Why would one person want to assume the responsibilities of labor, management, *and* ownership? Who needs those headaches?

Let's put the question to you. Why might *you* consider self-employment? (If you need help with your answer, take a peek at the five reasons we've listed below. Go ahead and look. We won't tell.)

BECAUSE YOU NEED YOUR INDEPENDENCE

Malcolm is a maverick and a free spirit, the kind of person who believes the most important things in life are freedom and independence. The guy who sees the eight-to-five workday—with its rush-hour traffic, cubicles, fluorescent lighting, committee meetings, and bosses—as a kind of prison. Malcolm's not what you'd call corporate material.

But that hasn't stopped him from building a successful career. Combining his talent for words and his passion for visiting new places, Malcolm makes his living as a travel writer. He's not getting rich, but he loves his job, and—most importantly—he works on his own terms.

Some people weren't born to work in a structured environment. It's that simple. For them, the predictability and routine of doing the same job, the same way, with the same people, under the same conditions, day in and day out, is intolerable. For others, the issue is authority. Some people bristle at the idea of taking orders from or reporting to another person. Call them rebels or do-it-yourselfers. Either way, they have a strong need to be their own bosses. For them, self-employment isn't an option; it's a necessity.

THE BIBLE SAYS

The Bible and Your Career Decision

God cares about your decisions.

The Bible says:
"I have commanded you, 'Be Strong and courageous! Don't tremble or be terrified, because the Lᴏʀᴅ your God is with you wherever you go' " (Joshua 1:9, God's Word).

BECAUSE YOU CAN'T STAND THE CORPORATE ENVIRONMENT

Four years into her career as a software designer for a large financial organization, Tabitha was making more money than her father ever did. And she was miserable. It's not that she hated her job. She loved designing software. Tabitha's problem had to do with the atmosphere at her company. For one thing, she felt stifled by corporate policy. Innovation and creativity weren't exactly prized commodities where Tabitha worked. Anything new or different was viewed with skepticism. As a result, Tabitha kept a lot of great ideas to herself.

Tabitha also struggled with the pressures of corporate life. Tight production schedules meant lots of overtime. Seventy- to eighty-hour work weeks were the norm rather than the exception. And with hundreds of thousands of dollars riding on the outcome of each project, failure was not an option. One missed deadline or critical mistake could spell doom for a career. Constant tension was a fact of life in Tabitha's office.

Bureaucracy was another of Tabitha's corporate pet peeves. Even the smallest decisions required committee meetings, market research, or statistical analysis. Tabitha once had to get permission from a supervisor to put a picture of her cat on her desk.

Most of all, though, Tabitha despised office politics. From back-stabbing coworkers to divisional power struggles, Tabitha hated having to constantly watch her back, never knowing whom to trust.

Her utter disgust with corporate life led Tabitha to strike out on her own. Two years ago she became a full-time consultant, working with several different companies on projects that required outside help. While she still works in office settings, as an independent contractor Tabitha doesn't have to concern herself with the ugly side of corporate life.

Obviously not all corporations are as bad as Tabitha's. But if you're going to work for a company, no matter what company you choose, you're going to have to deal with restrictions, pressure, bureaucracy, and office politics in one form or another. Some people thrive in an office setting. Others prefer not to load themselves down with corporate baggage, so they opt for self employment.

BECAUSE YOUR DREAM JOB DEMANDS IT

When Ellen was seventeen, she helped plan her sister's wedding. In the process, she stumbled onto a career. Helping her sister order flowers, interview caterers, schedule dress fittings, check out banquet halls, and contact churches gave Ellen a glimpse at some talents and abilities she didn't know she had.

A few weeks later, one of the teachers at school handed out a question-naire to help students identify their goals in life. Under the heading "Dream Job," Ellen jokingly wrote down "wedding coordinator." But the more she thought about it, the more she realized that her dream job might not be such a far-fetched idea after all.

Ellen started slow, treating wedding planning more as a hobby or a part-time job than a career. She coordinated a couple of friends' weddings and even went out-of-state to help with her cousin's wedding. Then things started to escalate. A neighbor asked Ellen to coordinate his daughter's wedding, and it turned out to be a tremendous success. At the reception, the bride thanked Ellen publicly and couldn't say enough good things about her work. Several guests at the wedding asked Ellen for her business card so that they could schedule her services.

That's when Ellen realized that she was staring at a career opportunity. The next week she had business cards printed up. She ran some ads in the local newspaper. She asked the caterers, seamstresses, and ministers with whom she did business to start recommending her services to the couples they talked to.

Like Malcolm, Ellen's not getting rich from her job, but she's able to support herself nicely. Her business has increased to the point that she's considering hiring someone to help her meet the demand!

If your career interests are out of the ordinary, you might consider self-employment. Dream jobs usually make the best careers. (But be smart about it. If you're 5'5" and your dream job is to play in the NBA, it's time to mosey on over to reality and rethink your career strategy.)

BECAUSE YOU WANT TO STAY CLOSE TO YOUR FAMILY

Jackie's number one priority is her family. When her first child was born, she left her job as a fourth-grade teacher to stay at home with him. But she didn't leave the working world. Instead, she became a tutor. Five days a week, Jackie hosts "learning parties" in her home for struggling students.

She helps them with their homework and spends extra time with them on the subjects they find most difficult.

Though she makes significantly less than she did as a teacher, Jackie's tutoring job provides an ideal second income for the family. Besides, money's not Jackie's main concern. By tutoring in her home, Jackie is able to spend quality time with her young son.

Studies have shown that nothing contributes to the well-being of a child more than consistent parental involvement in the child's life. Parents who sacrifice careers outside of the home for the sake of their families should be admired.

A wealth of self-employment opportunities are available for stay-at-home parents (or others who prefer to work close to their families). Illustrators, Web-site designers, seamstresses, accoun-

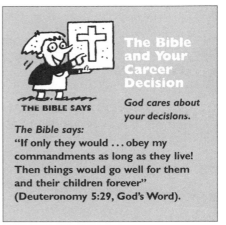

The Bible and Your Career Decision

THE BIBLE SAYS

God cares about your decisions.

The Bible says:
"If only they would ... obey my commandments as long as they live! Then things would go well for them and their children forever"
(Deuteronomy 5:29, God's Word).

tants, editors, and telemarketers have all carved out successful career niches at home, while at the same time providing vital support and nearness to their families. If your family is your top priority, chances are you'll be able to find a career to accommodate your needs.

BECAUSE YOU DON'T HAVE ANY OTHER CHOICE

For Carl, self-employment was a last resort. He'd never even thought about working for himself until he was riffed as a high school industrial arts teacher. (In teacher talk, R.I.F. stands for "reduction in force"; essentially it means being laid off.) With no other schools in the area hiring and relocation out of the question, Carl was faced with a dilemma. The only jobs available for which he was qualified didn't pay enough for him to support his wife and daughter. That's when Carl decided to give self-employment a shot.

Putting his industrial arts training to use, Carl hired himself out as a general handyman. He built some decks, dug a foundation or two, installed a set of windows, and even did some minor electrical and plumbing work. Then one day, a friend of Carl's father hired Carl to build and install kitchen cabinets in his home. The man was so pleased with the results that he asked Carl to make cabinets for other rooms in the house.

Word of mouth spread, and soon Carl had enough cabinet orders to justify purchasing new equipment and renting shop space. And, my, how things have snowballed since then! Today, Carl's cabinet business brings in millions of dollars in orders a year. Carl has more than twenty people working for him. What's more, he's seriously considering expanding his operation into other areas of construction. And while he's still not completely comfortable with being "the boss," Carl's finding that ownership has its privileges.

While desperation may not be the best reason for considering self-employment, it's important to remember that some of the best things in life are born through adversity. To put it in plain English, if you're at the end of your career rope, don't rule out self-employment as an option. You never know what might happen.

If the stories of Malcolm, Tabitha, Ellen, Jackie, and Carl strike a chord with you, you might want to give self-employment a second thought. The risks involved in working for yourself are considerable, but then, so are the rewards.

Self Employment at a Glance

The Pros and Cons of Working for Yourself

WIDE ANGLE

Pros   You decide when, where, and how you're going to do things.
You can hire anyone you choose.
You don't have to worry about someone taking credit for your work.
You, and not some boss, will reap the benefits of your work.
You don't have to worry about being fired or laid off.
You don't have to worry about getting caught goofing off on the job.
You don't have to worry about "kissing up" to your boss.
You have the potential to make a great deal of money.
You'll gain experience in many different areas.
You'll have a career that you can truly call your own.

Cons   You're looking at some serious hours on the job.
Your family may suffer while you try to get your business off the
    ground.
You're risking your financial future.
You'll have no one else to blame if things go wrong.
You're the one who's going to pay the price for any serious mistakes.
You'll need to familiarize yourself with all facets of your business.
You'll need to always stay informed on changes in the marketplace.
You'll have to pay for your own medical insurance, retirement plan, and
    expense account.
Your business will become a big part of your life, whether you like it or
    not.
You're likely to fail.

A DECLARATION OF INDEPENDENCE

HOW DO YOU BECOME SELF-EMPLOYED?

All right, so you think you've got what it takes to be self-employed. Now what? It's a long way from *wanting* to work for yourself to actually *working* for yourself. How do you get started? What steps does a person need to take in order to begin his own company? Depending on what you want to do, the steps will vary. But here are six things you'll probably need to consider, regardless of your choice.

CHOOSE YOUR START-UP METHOD

Generally there are 3 different ways to go into business for yourself: start your own company, buy an existing business, or buy a franchise. The first option, *starting a business from scratch,* is the riskiest. Only about 20 percent of all start-up businesses last more than 5 years. But if you're willing to face those risks, start-up businesses can bring you an awful lot of personal satisfaction, not to mention a nice chunk of change. Perhaps the best reason to consider a start-up business is that in creating it, you become intimately acquainted with every aspect of the company. The main drawback to a start-up company is the time and energy it takes not only to make people aware of your company, but to convince them to check you out.

The second self-employment option is *buying an existing business.* The good thing about buying a business is that, in a sense, a lot of the work has already been done for you. For example, it's likely that the business already has customers, so you won't be starting from scratch in marketing the company. It's also likely that the business also has a physical building and trained employees, saving you money and time, and freeing you up to concentrate on other areas. What's more, financing is usually easier to come by if you're buying an existing company. On the downside, buying someone else's business tends to restrict your options. While you can certainly make minor tweaks here and there, trying to make wholesale changes to the business to fit your ownership style is a recipe for disaster. The clientele of the business will probably expect things done in "traditional" ways. Any radical departure from that tradition could result in loss of business.

The third option is *buying a franchise.* Franchises exist in almost every area of retail. They're the "brand names" that people know and feel comfortable with. Think about it: when you see golden arches, you know exactly what to expect. That familiarity is part of the appeal in buying a franchise. You'll pay not only for the store, but for the parent company's expertise, it's "track record" in launching and sustaining successful stores. One of the benefits of a franchise is also its biggest drawback. Because practices and procedures are fairly consistent throughout the chain, all you'll really need to do is follow rules. The drawback is that the established procedures leave little room for personal freedom.

If you buy a franchise, the steps you'll need to take will be spelled out for you by the parent company, so there's no need for us to go into those details. For those of you who are considering starting a business or buying an existing one, here are some more tasks you'll need to consider.

EVALUATE YOUR FINANCIAL NEEDS

Obviously you'd love to get rich from your new business, and maybe that'll happen someday. But for now, you'll need to figure out how much money this business of yours must earn in order to support yourself (and your family). The best way to do this is to total up all of your monthly expenses—from groceries to utilities to credit cards to spending money. Some expenses will need to be converted into monthly sums. For example, if you're paying $600 a year in auto insurance, write it down as $50 a month. You may also need to estimate some expenses, such as auto repair and maintenance, clothing, and charitable donations. Be as complete as possible in your tally. The object is to find out just how much money it will take to sustain your present lifestyle (assuming that your present lifestyle is tolerable for you).

As a business owner, you should receive three types of financial reimbursement from your company: a salary that's competitive with that of other people at your level in your industry, a return on your initial investment, and cash flow to cover your business expenses and overhead.

IDENTIFY YOUR MARKET

The $64,000 question for any business owner is "Who's going to buy your products or services?" The double-or-nothing bonus question is "How do you get those people to actually part with their cash in exchange for what you have to offer?" Yes, future business owners, you've entered the wonderful world of marketing.

Note that the "how" question follows the "who" question. Before you determine *how* you're going to bring in business, you need to know *who* your potential customers are. And to answer the "who" question, you'll need to do some market research.

The most common way to do market research is through surveys, asking potential customers questions that will help you better understand them and their buying habits. Most surveys are done either by mail, over the phone, or in person. There are many ad agencies and marketing firms available to do research for you, but if you're a new business owner, it's recommended that you do the research yourself to get a hands-on feel for the market.

Before you start working on questions for the survey, you'll need to figure out what it is you want to discover from it. Here are some ideas to get you started.

- Why would someone buy what I have to offer?
- What is it about my business that will make people want to purchase what I offer?
- What is my customer profile? What age, sex, and income level am I targeting?
- How important is the location of my business?
- How much would a typical customer spend in a year for what I have to offer?
- What are the strengths and weaknesses of my competitors?

The questions you use in your survey should be specific to the products or services you offer. Regardless of what you're selling, though, you should keep a couple of tips in mind.

- Target only potential customers with your surveys. The opinions of people who will never buy your products or services should mean little to you (when it comes to business, that is).
- Make sure the survey questions are worded in such a way that you receive maximum benefit from the responses. Be as specific as possible.

Market research may sound like one giant hassle, but the more work you put into it, the better results you'll take away from it.

SECURE YOUR FINANCING

Once you've got some solid numbers from your market research, it's time to put together your business plan and secure financing for your new company. A business plan is simply a document that explains in detail your plans for the business and what you expect the business to do. Usually a business plan consists of three sections:

the operations plan, which explains the basics of the business like where it's located, what it does, and who works for it,

the marketing plan, which describes how the business will meet the needs of its customers (needs that were identified in your market survey) and maintain a satisfactory cash flow, and

the financial plan, which projects the future fiscal performance of the business.

THE BIBLE SAYS

The Bible and Your Career Decision

God cares about your decisions.

The Bible says:
"I'm leaving you peace. I'm giving you peace. I don't give you the kind of peace that the world gives. So don't be troubled or cowardly " (John 14:27, God's Word).

Business plans are necessary if you're going to need financing for your new business venture. Most banks and other lending institutions require that a plan be submitted before they'll even consider a business loan application.

And while we're on the subject of financing, remember that small business loans from banks are not the only source of money for a new company. If you own a house, you can use a home-equity loan to fund your start-up. If worse comes to worst, borrowing money from relatives, friends, and other personal acquaintances is another possibility.

Regardless of how you finance your new company, though, we strongly recommend that you create a business plan and use it to guide your decision-making.

MAKE YOURSELF KNOWN

Like it or not, you will be your company's own best marketer. As you go about your business, look for ways to spread the word about your new venture. Network like crazy. If possible, join some professional trade organizations. Make yourself known at Chamber of Commerce functions. Leave a stack of business cards with an associate at a cooperating company and ask him to recommend your business whenever possible. Look for networking potential in everyone you meet. If you're a small business owner, you should be promoting your company, sometimes subtly and sometimes overtly, 24-7 (24 hours a day, 7 days a week). After all, the owner's always on the clock.

LIFE, DEATH, AND TAXES

One more thing, don't forget that your Uncle in Washington is entitled to a percentage of your income. Tax rules vary enough and are confusing enough that we suggest you meet with a business banker or tax advisor *before* you start raking in the money. He or she may be able to help you outline what tax obligations you may have.

FINALLY

We've just scratched the surface in describing the work that goes into starting a business. The process takes more effort and time than you can possibly imagine. If you got tired just reading about starting a business, maybe self-employment's not for you. On the other hand, if the prospect of all that work appeals to you, you might want to give self-employment a shot.

THE INSIDE SCOOP

RESEARCHING COMPANIES YOU'RE INTERESTED IN

Would you buy a house without first looking at it carefully? Of course not. You'd want to walk through the place dozens of times to get a feel for it. You'd try to picture yourself living there. You'd gather information on taxes, utilities, and repair history. You'd bring in a professional inspector to check the place out. After all, if you're going to be spending most of your time in a place, you want to make sure that the place is right for you.

The same principle holds true for potential employers. If you're considering a career with a corporation, it makes sense to find out all you can about the company.

How, you ask? Keep reading.

FOLLOW THE DATA TRAIL

Perhaps the best place to start your investigation is online, at the company's web site. See what the company has to say about itself. Take note of how the site is designed. Is it creative and bold? Is it dull and lifeless? Is it sloppy and disorganized? Though it would be a mistake to base your entire opinion of the company on its web site, it's possible that the site *is* a reflection of what the company is really like. Just something to keep in mind.

If the company does not have a web site, place a call to its human resources department. Explain that you're interested in learning more about the company and ask them to send you as much information as possible about its history, policies, guidelines, and so forth. Many companies have brochures and packets of information ready for just such requests.

You should also peruse local newspapers, business magazines, and trade journals for the inside scoop on the company. Look for information such as whether the company is currently facing legal battles, how much it supports charitable organizations in the area, and how profitable it is.

While we're on the subject of profitability, it's also a good idea to chart the company's stock performance over an extended period of time. Make it a habit to check the business indexes in the newspaper each day. Don't concern yourself with minor fluctuations here and there. Such price changes mean very little in the long run. Instead, you'll want to watch for long-term trends, steady increases or declines in the stock value.

USE THE PERSONAL TOUCH

Talk to your networking contacts to see what they know about the company. It's possible that one or more of them has had business dealings with the organization. From their experiences, you may be able to get a sense of the company's reputation in the industry and in the community.

Your next step is to go straight to the source. Schedule an information interview with a manager in the company. Unless you know a manager personally, you'll probably need to contact the human resources department to schedule such an interview. Approach the interview as though you were an investigative journalist. Come prepared with a list of questions and get the information you need. Keep in mind, though, that the person you interview may be a valuable contact to you later in your job search, so treat her with respect.

Finally, your best research bet is to get to know a worker in the company, preferably someone in a position comparable to what you would be doing if you worked there. Invite this person to lunch (your treat) to talk informally about the company. Ask him what he likes about his job and what he doesn't like. Talk about what he perceives to be the strengths and weaknesses of the company. Assure him that everything he says will be kept confidential—and then make sure you keep it confidential!

PUT YOUR KNOWLEDGE TO USE

The information you gather about a company can serve you well in a job interview—assuming, of course, that you're still interested in the company after having researched it. The key is to demonstrate your knowledge of the corporation to the interviewer in a natural way. Don't start spouting obscure facts about the company and hope to make an impression. The last thing you want to do is come off as an obsessive nutjob with too much time on his hands.

If you're too obvious in your efforts to show off your knowledge of the company, you might as well tape a big sign on your back that reads, "I'm trying way too hard." Stay away from awkward attempts at transition ("Speaking of the advertising department, I'll bet you guys are *advertising* the fact that your stock has risen eight points in the last week.") Instead, look for natural openings in the conversation in which you can drop nuggets of your acquired information. If the natural openings aren't there, keep your mouth shut.

What's true for buying a house is true for researching potential employers: the more you know beforehand, the happier you'll be later.

BON VOYAGE?

What You Need to Know About International Jobs

Some call it the ultimate career experience. Others call it the worst mistake of their lives. Your point of view probably depends on your sense of adventure and your tolerance for less-than-ideal circumstances. The life of an expatriate and the challenge of working in a foreign country are certainly not for everyone. If you're considering an international job, there are some things you should know.

Beyond the Adventure

At the risk of bursting some bubbles, it's our duty to inform you that corporate life in a foreign country is not always an adventure of the enjoyable kind. If you're serious about considering foreign employment, you need to know the problems and difficulties that await you.

Obviously the first and most glaring problem is the language/culture barrier. You may think you have an idea of what it's like to be limited in your communicative abilities, but until you're thrown into such a situation, you can't imagine the frustration and helplessness that goes along with it. Conversation is reduced to a level reminiscent of a "Dick and Jane" book. ("We will meet tomorrow. You will read your report. I will read my report. We will talk about the reports.") And don't forget that it's you, as the foreigner, who makes such rudimentary conversation necessary. Unless you're remarkably fluent in the native language, you can expect problems to develop as a result of the language barrier.

You should also know that not all countries permit foreigners to receive work visas, preferring to fill positions with native citizens whenever possible.

Even the countries that do allow work visas may be reluctant to bring in foreign workers because of the expense involved.

Your best bet for securing an overseas position is to have actual business experience in your chosen country. You will need to convince potential employers that you know how to conduct business and handle clients in that country. You will also need to demonstrate an awareness and understanding of local customs and traditions.

Last, and certainly not least, if you plan to take family members overseas with you, you will need to consider their needs carefully. A year-long assignment for you may seem like a five-year ordeal to them.

THE WORLD AT YOUR FINGERTIPS

Okay, we're done with the discouraging stuff. Assuming you're still interested in an international position, we have one piece of advice for locating the information you'll need: Go online.

Depending on the country you've targeted and the job you're seeking, you should be able to find at least a dozen helpful sites with just a casual spin through cyberspace.

If you're looking for a departure point, you might try one or more of these sites:

World Wide Web Consortium
(www.w3.org/pub/DataSources/WWW/Servers.html)
Arranged alphabetically by continent and then by country, this list includes most of the web servers in each country. Usually the lists are conveniently categorized—"business," "commercial," "education," and so on. The only problem is that most of the sites use their native language, so if you're not fluent, you may need a translator.

CityNet

(www.city.net.com)
This site is connected to over 5,000 locations around the world, many of which provide information on local business and employment opportunities.

Argus Clearinghouse

(www.clearinghouse.net)
This collection of online resource guides includes many international sites in its "Business and Employment" section.

PARLEZ VOUS RÉSUMÉ?

Once you've made the necessary contacts with international corporations, the next step is to send out your résumé. No problem, right? You just stick a little more postage on your existing résumé and ship it out to the interested parties overseas. Isn't that the way it works?

Not if you actually want to *get the job*.

Have you considered translating your résumé? The standard American format for résumés may not work abroad. For example, some countries prefer citizenship and passport information on the *curricula vitae* (as résumés are known internationally). Language skills are held in high regard, so the vitae must be exceptionally well-written.

European corporations often request a handwritten cover letter from applicants so that they can judge neatness and grammar. They may also submit the letter for handwriting analysis, which they then use in lieu of a personal profile. In Asia, the emphasis is on schooling, so you're required to list every school you've attended—all the way back to kindergarten.

Your best course of action, then, is to enlist the services of a reputable translation agency. The ideal agency will use an accredited translator, an editor, and a proofreader to shape your résumé as needed.

THE MATCH GAME

HOW WELL WOULD YOU FIT IN AT YOUR CHOSEN COMPANY?

You'd think that it would be enough to find a company that has a position open for someone with your skills and background. You'd think that negotiating a mutually agreeable salary is the final consideration before accepting the job. You'd be making a big mistake.

If you're seriously considering a position with a company, you're going to need to do some "chemistry experiments" first. Leave the test tubes at home, though. We're talking about personal chemistry—how well your personality, tendencies, and preferences mesh with the people you'd be working with and the environment you'd be working in.

WHAT YOU'LL NEED TO KNOW

When you visit the company, keep your eyes peeled for clues as to what it's like. First, consider the pace of life in the office. Are people hurrying around all the time? Are phones ringing everywhere? Does chaos reign? If so, how does that fit your personality? Do you thrive in chaotic situations? Or would you be staring a nervous breakdown in the face after a week or two?

If, on the other hand, the office has all the vibrancy and energy of a mausoleum, you'll need to consider that as well. How well could you work in library-like environment? Would such a setting help you concentrate better on your work? Or would it cause you to drift into deep slumber?

You'll also want to get a sense of the interpersonal relationships in the company. Is the atmosphere thick with tension and deadlines? If so, don't expect a warm and friendly vibe among the employees. If, however, you see people chatting in the halls and greeting each other when they pass, you can probably conclude that the company encourages interaction among its employees. You'll need to decide the kind of corporate atmosphere you prefer.

WHO YOU'LL NEED TO TALK TO

In order to get an accurate sense of what a company is like, you'll need to talk to several different people.

Human Resources Representative

The human resources department is the "face" of the company, if you will. You can tell a lot about a corporation by the people in human resources. How helpful are they in directing your interviews? Do you get a sense that they're genuinely interested in you? Remember, if you have problems or needs as an employee, you're going to have to deal with human resources.

Your Future Boss

It's not out of line to ask a supervisor, "What kind of a manager are you?" or "What kind of people do well under your supervision?" But be sure to "listen between the lines" to his answer.

If he says something like, "I expect my people to work as hard as I do," you're probably dealing with a demanding boss. There's nothing wrong with that. Some people prefer a boss who monitors them closely. They're uncomfortable with too much freedom. If that's how you are, you might fit in well in the department.

If the boss says something like, "I prefer to work with self-motivated people," he's probably more of a hands-off supervisor, the kind who gives his employees a great deal of freedom. It's also likely that he's slightly removed from the people who work under him. If you're a person who thrives on constant attention and reassurance, you may have difficulty working with such a manager.

Your Future Co-workers

You don't have to form an immediate bond with everyone in the division. And it's not as though all your coworkers are automatically going to become your best friends. You will, however, be spending a great deal of time with these people. It's important that you be able not only to get along with them, but to be productive with them as a team.

As best you can, try to gauge the morale of the workers you talk to. To borrow a phrase usually associated with postal employees, are they a disgruntled bunch? Is their first instinct to say something positive or negative about the company? Do they seem to enjoy what they do? Do they seem

This is important

DON'T FORGET

Don't base your opinion of the company on a bad encounter with one person. One bad apple doesn't necessarily spoil the whole bunch. Make your decision based on your collective experience and your gut reaction.

The question you need to ask yourself is simple: Is this a place where I could be happy working day in and day out? Don't assume that you can adjust your personality and preferences to fit a company with which you are clearly ill-matched. No matter how good the job is or how much money you'll be making, chances are that in a few short months you'll be miserable.

God created you with a unique pattern of internal wiring, a one-of-a-kind set of personality traits, preferences, and abilities. You honor Him when you take your "internal wiring" into consideration in your job search. While there may not be one perfect job out there for you, there are jobs that will suit your unique personality. Don't sell yourself short and accept anything less.

excited at the prospect of working with you?

DON'T BE A BARGAIN

NEGOTIATING YOUR STARTING SALARY

The interview has been a smashing success. It's obvious to the interviewer that you're perfect for the job, and it's obvious to you that the job is perfect for you. So it's a done deal, right? Not so fast, Sparky. There's still the matter of cash to consider.

It seems that both you and the company have a certain salary in mind for the position. Would you care to guess whose figure is higher? That's not to say the numbers are radically different. They're in the same ballpark, but one is sitting in the left-field bleachers, and the other is behind home plate.

It's negotiating time.

Few people actually enjoy haggling with others. Most people find it to be a pain in the posterior. But in the business world, negotiating skills are necessary for survival. If you haven't been taught these skills yet, it's time you learned. So before you enter into negotiations about your salary with the hiring manager, here are a few tips you should consider.

KNOW YOUR SITUATION

The first thing you need to do is honestly assess yourself. Do your skills and experience make you an ideal candidate for the job? Is there something about you that sets you apart from the other candidates? Are your skills in demand in the corporate world? If you answered yes to these questions, you've got leverage.

Leverage is good.

Another thing to consider is the job market. If you're interviewing in a tight job market, you're more likely to negotiate yourself a better deal. It's the law of supply and demand. If there's a short supply of qualified job applicants, demand increases. In order to land a qualified applicant, a company might be willing to offer a signing bonus, extra vacation time, or a flexible work-at-home arrangement. In mathematical terms, the equation would look something like this:

$$\text{Tight job market} = \text{More leverage for you}$$

Leverage gives you the confidence to say to yourself, "If this company doesn't meet my salary requirements, there are others that will." It also gives you the confidence to decline the company's initial salary offer if it's not what you think it should be.

One word of caution here: Before you start trying to use leverage in an interview situation, make sure you have leverage to use. Don't make the mistake of overestimating your worth. What if you decline an offer and then discover that no second offer is forthcoming? That would be a rather embarrassing way to find out that you're not quite as valuable as you thought you were.

ARM YOURSELF WITH FACTS

Don't just *tell* the hiring manager that the salary offer is too low, *prove* it. Produce clear evidence that your price is in line with the market or with the salaries of employees in similar positions at the company. Equip yourself with relevant facts, figures, charts, and graphs to back up your claims.

Where do you find such information? Start with the Internet. You can find all kinds of comparative salary data online. (Need a place to start? Try *wageweb.com,* which provides regularly updated salary information on hundreds of careers.) Your next stop should be the newspaper. Many want ads include salary information. And if all else fails, try the personal touch. Talk to current and former employees. While they may be reluctant to share their own salary specifics, they may have information that will help you.

Arming yourself with facts will serve two purposes. First, it will demonstrate to the hiring manager that you've done your homework and make it harder for him to justify a lower salary offer. Second, it will reassure you that your demands are not unreasonable.

PLAY YOUR CARDS RIGHT

What's true in deodorant commercials is true in salary negotiations: you should "never let them see you sweat." The quickest way to end a negotiation is to appear impatient or greedy. That's why it's recommended that you delay serious salary discussion until the final stages of an interview.

It's also recommended that you get a general idea of the salary range for the position from the start. This will give you a clearer sense of how much room you have to maneuver.

Finally, don't make the mistake of accepting an offer too quickly. Some hiring managers may make you feel like you're in an automobile dealership. They won't let you leave without making a decision. You should know, though, that there is absolutely nothing wrong with asking for some time— usually a day—to think and pray about the offer.

Hiring managers aren't known for their benevolence. Few, if any, of them are going to volunteer to give you extra cash or perks. If you're not satisfied with a salary offer, it's your responsibility to make your feelings known. Ask for what you want, whether it's a signing bonus, extra vacation time, or a work-at-home arrangement. You may get turned down, but if you're a valuable enough prospect, you'll probably receive a counteroffer that's more to your liking. Therein lies the beauty of negotiation.

SECTION 3

KEEPING A JOB

LIFE IN THE REAL WORLD

ANTICIPATING WORKPLACE DEMANDS

"When I was a child, I talked like a child, I thought like a child, I reasoned like a child. When I became a man, I put childish ways behind me." (1 Corinthians 13:11)

The apostle Paul was speaking of spiritual maturity, but his words also have tremendous application to the business world. When you enter the workplace for the first time as a "career person," it's time to put childish ways behind you. If you want to be taken seriously—if you're interested in building not only a career, but a reputation you can be proud of—you will put away the childish attitudes, beliefs, and actions that marked your early years. That's not to say you can't have fun in the office or even get a little goofy on occasion. But you must keep in mind that you're standing on a new stage.

Gone are the days when people would laugh at your unpredictability and encourage your irresponsible behavior. Now you're in a venue where people appreciate the finer points of your personality. And you need to make sure that those finer points are showing.

The process of putting away childish things can be tough. In order to make the transition somewhat easier, we've compiled a list of tips in the form of ten qualities you'll need to develop that should help you build a successful, "grown up" career.

Note: We're not writing for David Letterman, so this is *not* a top ten list. These qualities aren't ranked according to importance.

Professional Demeanor

What's wrong with this picture? The first day in your new office, a client walks in with a question about his account. You stand up, high-five the guy, and say, "Yo, 'sup, my brotha?"

Sure, it's an extreme example, but it illustrates a rather obvious, and important, fact about life in the office. It's not the same as life at home. The rules are different. The attitudes are different. Interaction between people is different. It's more formal, more . . . well, businesslike. The proper greeting in a business setting includes a warm handshake, solid eye contact, and a respectful manner.

Not only should you maintain a business-like approach in your dealings with other people, you should carry that professional manner over into the way you dress. You may be new to the business world, but you don't have to look like it. Invest in a wardrobe that will help others see you the way you want to be seen in a business setting. If you want to be taken seriously by those who work around you, dress like it.

This is important: For a while, your new office demeanor is going to feel fake, as though you're pretending to be someone you're not. That's okay. It doesn't mean you're a phony. It means you're maturing and putting away childish attitudes.

An Eye for the Big Picture

This is not only the most important quality for someone new to the business world to master, it's also the one that takes longest to develop. An eye for the big picture means you are able to see beyond the scope of your own responsibilities, beyond even that of your office or division. The big picture is the entire panorama of your company's existence.

A big picture view is the opposite of the "tunnel vision" that tends to exist in most offices. Tunnel vision is the ability to see only what is directly in front of you or only what affects you. When you recognize that your contributions to the company must be joined with the contributions of others (whether it be marketing, sales, accounting, or any other division) before they take on any real value, you tend to develop a more accurate self-image and a greater appreciation for others in the workplace.

An eye for the big picture allows you to think in terms of what's best for the project or what's best for the company instead of what's best for you. Sometimes a big picture view means admitting that someone else is better suited to perform a task or take charge of a project. A big picture view allows you to see with clear-eyed realism your own strengths and weaknesses, as well as the strengths and weaknesses of your co-workers. It involves selecting the right people for the right tasks, regardless of who gets the glory. To put it in baseball terms, people who have an eye for the big picture are willing to "take one for the team"—that is, sacrifice personal glory for the sake of the end result.

Punctuality

In theory, this is perhaps the easiest quality to understand and develop. If your workday starts at eight, you should be in your office, ready to work, by . . . well, eight. What could be simpler, right? Well, for some people, juggling chain saws.

Call it passive-aggressive behavior, absentmindedness, laziness, or irresponsibility, but some people find it next to impossible to be on time for anything. But is that really such a big deal? After all, what's fifteen minutes here or there? The only thing that matters is that the work gets done, right?

Actually "fifteen minutes here or there" *is* a big deal. Total it up and those 15 minutes a day add up to about 3,675 minutes a year (based on 245 workdays—5 days a week for 49 weeks). Break it down and you get just over

61 hours a year. Break it down one more time and you come up with over seven-and-a-half days—more than a week of work missed, 15 minutes at a time.

The next question is, as long as the work gets done, who cares about what time you stroll into the office? The answer: your co-workers. Oh, it's not like they're going to say anything to your face about it. They may not even complain to each other. But you can bet they're thinking, *If she can come to work late, why can't I?* And that's where the problems begin. Do the math on the number of work hours lost if everyone in the office starts showing up fifteen minutes late.

Of course, maybe you're staying an extra fifteen minutes at the end of the day. In that case, no work time is actually lost and everything's okay, right?

Well . . . no. You see, chronic tardiness sends all kinds of messages to the people around you. It says, "I'm not responsible enough to manage my time properly." It says, "An extra fifteen minutes of sleep in the morning is more important to me than my responsibilities at work." It says, "I'm trying to get away with as much as I can in the office." Are those really the signals you want to send out?

We're not going to insult your intelligence by suggesting ways for you to get to work on time. You know what it is that's making you late. And you know how to correct it. The question is, are you willing to do that?

Attention to Detail

Paying attention to detail is dirty work. Few people enjoy it; few people make it a priority. For most people, "good enough" is good enough ("The report's not perfect, but it's good enough.") Some people leave the details to others ("I didn't have all the figures, so I just plugged in last year's numbers; I figure someone will catch it before it goes to the client.") Don't be one of those people. Take responsibility for making sure that your work is the best it can be.

At the risk of sounding like your junior high English teacher, we implore you to proofread everything that goes out with your name on it—from e-mail correspondence to year-end reports. Check for grammar, punctuation, and spelling mistakes. Don't associate yourself with sloppy or halfhearted work.

An attention to detail says to others, "I care about my work and my reputation. I'm not satisfied with 'good enough,' and I don't need to rely on others to fix my mistakes."

Here's a tip, free of charge: You put together attention to detail and an eye for the big picture, and you've got yourself a killer combination— the kind of combination people (meaning bosses) take notice of.

Going the Extra Mile

"Going the extra mile" for a person is one of the best ways to demonstrate your Christian faith in the office. It's also one of the best ways to gain the respect and gratitude of your coworkers.

That Extra Mile

DON'T FORGET

"If someone forces you to go one mile, go with him two miles" (Matthew 5:41).

Going the extra mile is simply giving people more than they expect. Let's say a co-worker comes to you with a question about a computer procedure. Your first instinct may be to give her a short answer and get back to work. What would happen instead if you took the time to leave your desk, go to her computer, and walk her through the process? It's a small sacrifice on your part, but it would probably mean a great deal to your co-worker.

We're not suggesting that you sacrifice your own job to help others do theirs. What we are suggesting is that whenever possible, you take the time to fully understand the problems of your co-workers and then take part in helping them solve those problems. If you don't have the answers a person is looking for, do some investigating to find out who does. Later, follow up with a phone call to the person to make sure the problem was solved.

Going the extra mile does *not* involve doing other people's work for them. It involves helping them develop the problem-solving skills they need to do the work themselves.

Team Spirit

You don't have to develop a buddy-buddy relationship with your co-workers. It doesn't really matter whether you like them as friends or not. But you have to get along them. More importantly, you have to develop a strong working relationship with them.

Bonus Point

CATCH A CLUE

One of the happy results of going the extra mile for other people is that you establish a mutual loyalty. You'll find that if you're willing to make an extra effort on someone's behalf, that person will reciprocate and go the extra mile for you when you need it.

Many professional sports teams are made up of players who can't stand each other. Yet they pull together for a common goal. The same should hold true for you and your co-workers. You may not have much to do with each other outside of the office, but when you're at work, you should put personal differences aside and function as a team. Meshing personalities is the key. One of the challenges of an office environment is learning to tolerate and interact with all kinds of personality types.

If you work with a large group of people, chances are that at least one of them is a jerk. You know who he is. He irritates you, he tries to press your buttons just to see how you'll react, and he'd probably stab you in the back if given half a chance. But he's a co-worker, and he's part of your team.

The truth is, you're going to encounter a lot of jerks throughout your career. The sooner you learn how to deal with them—and, more importantly, how to work with them—the better off you'll be. Jerks are not an endangered species in the corporate jungle.

Being a member of a team requires you to resolve or set aside petty differences and personality clashes with your teammates and work with them toward a common goal.

Dependability

If it's true that you're only as good as your word, how good are you? How much weight does your word carry in your office? If you say you're going to do something, do people automatically assume that you'll do it? Or do they roll their eyes and say, "Yeah, I've heard that one before."

Don't make promises you can't keep. Don't try to make yourself look good for a few moments at the expense of your reputation. If you know you can't get something done on time, don't tell your boss you can. If that means getting yelled at, accept the consequences and move on—with your reputation intact.

If you say something *will* be done on time, be prepared to move heaven and earth to get it done. Don't look for reasons to excuse you from your word ("I would have finished it on time if. . . ."). Look for ways to keep your word golden.

Ideally that dependability should carry over to your relationships with your co-workers. They should be able to depend on you for comfort in tough times. They should be able to depend on you for a smile at just the right time. And most importantly, they should be able to depend on you for the truth. If you can be counted on to respond honestly in all situations, you will emerge as a trusted, valued member of the office team.

Grace under Pressure

The corporate world is a hotbed of intense scrutiny and pressing deadlines. Some people wilt under the bright lights of tight scheduling and impatient bosses; others thrive. Regardless of which kind of person you are, you should work to maintain a certain amount of grace under pressure.

There will be times when you get angry, times when you feel like crying, times when you feel persecuted, and times when you want to quit. There's nothing wrong with any of those feelings. They're all perfectly normal responses to stress. Let yourself experience those emotions without feeling guilty about them. They will pass.

What you do need to guard against, though, is passing along the pressure you're feeling to others. Don't let your stress disrupt your co-workers. Don't take your anger out on them. Don't vent your steam in their direction.

Important point: This is *not* to say that you should keep your feelings to yourself. Don't let the stress eat away at you from the inside. Find a proper release for the pressure you're experiencing. Ideally a caring spouse or a best friend would be available to listen patiently while you vent your frustrations and share your feelings. If that's not the case for you, you might want to talk to a professional counselor.

Grace under pressure does not mean pretending that you're not feeling stress. It means finding the right way to deal with the pressure, a way that does not injure or negatively affect someone else.

Prioritizing

You've got ten things that need to be done by tomorrow. If you work through lunch and put in six or seven hours of overtime, you should be able to finish . . . five of them. But which five? And what will you tell the people waiting for the five you don't finish?

No one's going to walk into your office and number the assignments one through ten so that you'll know which ones to do first. That responsibility is all yours.

Prioritizing is usually learned through trial and error. It takes experience to recognize which things need to be done yesterday and which ones can wait until tomorrow. But here are some tips that may help.

First, it's unlikely that ten new things will be plopped down on your desk at the same time, each with a twenty-four hour deadline. Usually what happens is one or two surprise assignments will find their way to your desk, interfering with the three or four other assignments already on your schedule. Your task then is to figure out which assignment takes precedence. The best way to find that out is to ask. When somebody—usually your boss— hands you an assignment and says, "I need this right away," it's okay for you to say, "Right now I'm working on that presentation for the sales conference on Tuesday. Do you want me to drop that and start this?" Don't complain and don't argue. Just find out from your boss which assignment he thinks should take priority.

It's also a good idea to work ahead whenever possible on long-term assignments, so that when emergency assignments pop up, you can turn your attention to them without getting behind schedule on your other work.

Okay, that about does it. Do you feel overwhelmed? We wouldn't blame you if you do. There are a lot of skills to master in the workplace. The good news is that there's no deadline for developing these qualities. You can take things slowly, concentrating on one quality at a time. But the more effort you put into improving yourself and your workplace performance, the more positive results you're going to see.

THE SCOURGE OF THE WORKPLACE

SEXUAL HARASSMENT

Everyone deserves the right to work in an environment free of offensive encounters and threatening situations. Unfortunately, in many offices around the country that's not possible. For many women—and not a few men—going to the office every day is a traumatic experience. The cause of this grief is sexual harassment. And though many people may prefer to dismiss the claims of sexual harassment victims, the problem is real and it must be addressed.

WHAT THE LAW SAYS

In legal terms, sexual harassment is actually a form of discrimination. As such, it clearly violates Title VII of the Civil Rights Act of 1964, making it a punishable offense.

Actions that may be interpreted as sexual harassment include unwelcome sexual advances, requests for sexual favors, and verbal or physical conduct of a sexual nature.

Sexual harassment occurs if . . .

- submission to or rejection of these actions affects an individual's employment, whether explicitly or implicitly;
- it unreasonably interferes with an individual's work performance;
- it creates an intimidating, hostile, or offensive work environment.

Put simply, if the conditions of your job depend on going along with the offensive behavior, you're dealing with unlawful sexual harassment.

That's what the law says about sexual harassment. But if you're entering the workplace, there are some other things you need to know about the subject.

Sexual harassment victims are not always women.

Reports of men being harassed in the workplace are not uncommon. In that same vein, men are not always the accused in sexual harassment cases. Some women have been found guilty of harassment. Sexual harassment does not always involve members of the opposite sex. Same-sex harassment cases are becoming more and more common.

The sexual harasser does not necessarily have to be the victim's supervisor.

The person may be an agent of the supervisor (perhaps an assistant), a manager in another area, a co-worker, or even a nonemployee of the company. Unlawful sexual harassment does not necessarily have to involve economic injury or dismissal of the victim.

The victim does not necessarily have to be the person who was harassed.

Anyone who is affected by the offensive conduct may be the victim of sexual harassment.

Sexual harassment can only occur if the harasser's conduct is unwelcome.

The law is designed to protect people from sexual harassment. If you are a victim, you need to seek protection and relief. It's your right and your responsibility.

WHAT TO DO IF YOU'RE A VICTIM

Reluctance to report sexual harassment is one of the leading problems in the fight against it. No one wants to be thought of as prudish or overly sensitive, someone who "can't take a joke." And for that reason, victims tend to keep their mouths shut and silently endure the harassment. It should not be that way.

If you've experienced unwanted behavior at work, whether it be suggestive comments about your appearance, inappropriate touching or other physical contact, sexual jokes or comments, sexual advances, or exposure to sexually explicit materials, you must not keep that experience to yourself. It's unfair to you, and it's unfair to other people in the office who may be experiencing similar treatment. It's time to break your silence and make the harassment known.

Your first course of action should be to confront the harasser directly and make it clear to the person that the conduct is unwelcome and must stop. If that approach works and the harassment stops, you will have avoided a potentially messy situation. If, however, the situation does not resolve itself, you need to report the behavior to a superior.

If your boss is the one who's harassing you, you'll need to go to someone you can trust. If you're not comfortable going to your boss's boss, go to human resources. It's likely that someone there is trained to handle such situations and can tell you what you need to do.

Should you need to pursue the matter further, you may file charges of sexual harassment at any field office of the United States Equal Employment Opportunity Commission. Field offices are located in fifty cities throughout the United States. These offices are listed in most local telephone directories under "U.S. Government."

You should know that when the Equal Employment Opportunity Commission investigates allegations of sexual harassment, it looks at the whole record: the nature of the harassment, the circumstances surrounding the harassment, and the context in which the alleged unwanted advances were made. A judgment is then made on the allegations, based on the specific facts of the case.

If a ruling is made in your favor, you have further options to consider. If it is found that you have been discriminated against on the basis of sex, you are entitled to be placed in the position you would have been in if the discrimination had never occurred. Depending on your situation, you may be entitled to hiring, promotion, reinstatement, back pay, and other remuneration. You may also be entitled to damages to cover mental anguish and inconvenience. What's more, you may be in line for punitive damages if it is found that your employer acted with malice or reckless indifference. Finally, you may be entitled to attorney's fees.

Most importantly, if you are the victim of sexual harassment, you need to turn to the Lord in prayer. Ask for His comfort and healing, as well as His guidance and strength in the often-difficult road that lies ahead.

HOW TO MAINTAIN A HARASSMENT-FREE WORK ENVIRONMENT

Your grandmother probably told you that an ounce of prevention is worth a pound of cure. And though you may not have known what she was talking about when you were younger, her advice rings true for corporations seeking to eliminate sexual harassment in their workplaces.

Quite simply, prevention is the best tool for getting rid of sexually inappropriate behavior in the office. Employers must take the necessary steps to prevent sexual harassment from occurring. The logical first step is to educate employees. Workers must be made to understand what kinds of behavior will not be tolerated.

But the solution does not rest merely with management. Employees should look out for each other, offering support and a listening ear whenever harassment is suspected. Sometimes the most helpful thing a person can do for a victim of sexual harassment is to be available. The stigma attached to being a victim and the whispers and gossip that go along with any sex-related issue can be unbearable. Friends are needed.

So-called "gray areas" should also be addressed by the employees. Some actions may not quite qualify as sexual harassment, but may still make people uncomfortable nonetheless. These actions are usually categorized as "harmless fun." Sometimes, though, harmless fun is a slippery slope leading to harassment. So our advice to those who promote "harmless fun" in the office is . . . when in doubt, don't.

There's no need to tell off-color jokes in the work setting. There's no reason to talk about the steamy video someone else watched last night. There's no need to tell a co-worker how "really, really hot" she looks. What you do on your own time is between you and God. What you do in the office may be construed as sexual harassment.

One other point here: sexual harassers exist in a company only because others allow them to get away with their behavior. Would you believe it's possible that you may be helping to promote sexual harassment in your office without even realizing it? Do you laugh at sex jokes? Do you listen when someone tells you about a movie sex scene? Do you chuckle at double entendres? Do you encourage sexual inappropriateness in your office by your refusal to take a stand?

If so, it's a problem you should address. To borrow a slogan from another cause: if you're not part of the solution, you're part of the problem. People are being hurt by your refusal to act. Don't contribute to sexual harassment in the workplace—either by your actions or your inaction.

IT'S NOT FAIR

JOB DISCRIMINATION

Most of us would like to believe that, in a nation built on the principles of democracy and liberty for all, we are capable of treating everyone fairly, judging people solely on their words and actions. We'd like to believe that promotion and advancement, both in the workplace and in society in general, are the natural results of hard work and sacrifice. We'd like to believe that no one is hindered by or treated differently because of physical characteristics.

We'd also like to believe in Santa Claus, the Easter Bunny, and infomercial claims—but we can't.

Instead, we're left to make do in our imperfect world—a world in which discrimination is far too common. In fact, unless you fit a very narrow physical profile—the "right" gender, race, age, and physical makeup—you face a very real possibility of being discriminated against, in one form or another, in the workplace. Does that surprise you? Would you know what to do in the face of discrimination? Let's get to the heart of this controversial issue.

WHAT IS DISCRIMINATION?

Discrimination occurs when two or more people in similar situations are treated differently because of a personal bias or prejudice. Federal law forbids discrimination based on race, sex, pregnancy, religion, age, national origin, disability, or union activity. Recent laws have been enacted to include marital status and sexual preference on this list.

We should point out, though, that preferential treatment is not the same as discrimination, at least not in the eyes of the court. Nepotism, showing favoritism to family members and close friends, is not a violation of discrimination laws. It's an infuriating and unfair practice, but it's not illegal. Bosses get away with it all the time.

HOW DO YOU KNOW IF YOU'RE A VICTIM?

You may be saying to yourself, "I'm still a little fuzzy on the difference between nepotism and discrimination, so how am I supposed to know whether I've been discriminated against?" Ask yourself four questions (this is what's known as the McDonnell-Douglas Test):

1. Are you a member of a "protected class"? That is, you meet criteria set down in the six major pieces of legislation that address discrimination? In plain English: Is the discrimination you're facing based on race, sex, religion, national origin, age, disability, or a medical condition?

2. Were you qualified for the position in question? Did you have the necessary training, license, or credentials?

3. Did your employer take action against you? Were you fired or demoted?

4. Were you replaced by someone who isn't in your protected class?

A positive response to these four questions may suggest a legitimate claim of discrimination. But proving discrimination in a court of law is not an easy task. In addition to the McDonnell-Douglas Test, you'll need to consider several other factors. For example, how blatant or obvious was the discrimination you experienced? Were any rude or derogatory comments directed toward you or your protected class? Does your employer have a history of bias or prejudice, especially toward your protected class?

HOW DO YOU RESOLVE THE MATTER?

In cases of discrimination, the best course of action often is a settlement between the victim and the company, achieved through negotiation and mediation. In a settlement, the victim agrees to give up the case against the company in exchange for a modest sum. Though it may sound like a less-than-desirable way to conclude matters, in most instances, it is preferable to a courtroom trial.

If you prefer to pursue the matter further, you may file an official "charge of discrimination" with the Equal Employment Opportunity Commission (EEOC). The charge must be filed within 180 days of the discriminatory act. The EEOC will then conduct a lengthy and thorough investigation into the charge. The prospects beyond the

Something You Should Know

CATCH A CLUE

If you have been discriminated against unlawfully, you are entitled to a settlement that will put you in the position you would have been in if the discrimination had never occurred. Depending on your circumstances, you may be entitled to hiring, promotion, reinstatement, back pay, and other funds. You may also be entitled to damages to compensate you for future financial losses, mental anguish, and inconvenience. And remember, you may also be entitled to attorney's fees.

investigation are a bit grim, though. In 90 percent of the cases it investigates, the EEOC finds no probable cause for discrimination.

It is our fervent hope that you never experience discrimination in the workplace. If you do, however, please seek help through the proper channels. Chances are you're not the only person in the company being victimized by the discrimination. Remember, everyone has the right to prosper and advance in his or her career. When that right is taken away, something must be done.

READING IS FUNDAMENTAL . . . TO CAREER SUCCESS

STAYING INFORMED THROUGH INDUSTRY-RELATED PERIODICALS

One of the keys to success in any career is continuing education. But not all learning takes place in a classroom or workshop. "Mini-textbooks," in the form of trade, technical, and professional journals are relatively inexpensive means for staying abreast of developments in your field.

AN ACQUIRED TASTE

We're going to let you in on a little secret. But if anybody asks you about it, you didn't hear it from us. Got it? Okay, here's the secret. When you first start looking at trade journals or technical magazines, you'll probably find them about as interesting as bran cereal. Most professional journals aren't known for their peppy writing and attention-grabbing topics. In fact, most of what you read at first won't make a whole lot of sense to you. The technical jargon and industry shorthand will seem like gobbledygook to you. And the stuff that does make sense to you—the comings, goings, and achievements of people in the industry you've never heard of—you won't care much about. But, like a foreign language, the more you study these periodicals and immerse yourself in them, the clearer the technical jargon and industry shorthand will become to you. If you make a concerted effort to peruse these journals regularly, reading even the most boring and technical articles, your career will benefit.

WHY READ THEM?

The primary benefit that trade journals offer professionals is a glimpse of the industry's "big picture." For all the diversity that exists in your profession, trade magazines help you see the common threads that bind you to other workers in the industry. You can read about the problems, struggles, solutions, and achievements of others in your profession and apply what you learn to your career.

By keeping up on what's current in your profession and what's on the horizon (a popular topic in most professional journals), you can stay ahead of the curve in spotting trends before they fully emerge and recognizing practical applications for new technologies, methods, or ideologies. What's more, by reading about the comings and goings of other people in the industry, you may get a better sense as to the trajectory of your own career.

The Bible and Your Career Decision

God cares about your decisions.

THE BIBLE SAYS

The Bible says:
"The Lord is my helper. I will not be afraid. What can mortals do to me?" (Hebrews 13:6, God's Word).

LET THE SUITS PICK UP THE BILL

Many companies (or departments within a company) have a budget set aside specifically for magazine and periodical subscriptions. Talk to your supervisor to see if that's the case with your company. If so, submit to your supervisor a list of two or three trade publications that you would like the company to subscribe to and make available to you. Chances are your request will be granted without a fuss. You may even be commended for taking the initiative in furthering your education. (Yeah, right. And then you might be named chairman of the board later that same day. Get real.)

If your company (or department) does not have a budget for magazine subscriptions, you may still be able to wrangle a subscription or two for yourself. You'll probably need to list a few compelling reasons for the company to grant your request. If so, concentrate on the benefits the *company* will reap from the investment. Find a useful or enlightening article in one of the periodicals, tear it out, and then list some ways that the insight of the article may be applied to improve working conditions or productivity at your company. Show your boss the article and the list. Remember, the worst he can do is say no. (Actually, the worst he could do is say no and then fire you for making such an outlandish request. But that's not likely to happen.)

Learning on the job is part of any fulfilling career. Don't pass up any opportunities to learn more about your profession—even if the information is buried between the pages of an industry journal.

STRENGTH IN NUMBERS

JOINING A PROFESSIONAL ORGANIZATION

Few things in life are as frustrating as a stale and stagnant career. We're not talking about the boredom that comes from a lack of work. Chances are you're not suffering from a lack of things to do. And we're not talking about being stalled on the corporate ladder. Even people on the top rungs are not immune to a stale career.

We're talking about the stagnation that comes from the lack of challenge, the slight brain numbness that results from working on the same type of projects and interacting with the same people day in and day out.

The problem may not be a bad career choice or boredom with work. The problem may be a limited circle of professional acquaintances and opportunities. The remedy, then, would be to increase one's social contacts, professionally speaking. One way to do this is to join a professional organization in your industry.

MEMBERSHIP HAS ITS PRIVILEGES

Maybe you're not the joining type. Fine. But before you dismiss the idea of becoming a member of a professional organization, you owe it to yourself to find out what that organization could do for you.

The first and most obvious benefit of joining a professional organization is being put into contact with hundreds, maybe thousands, of other people in your line of work. Many of these people will have faced the same problems you face, dealt with the same kinds of clients you deal with, and wondered about the same questions you wrestle with. You would have access to some very bright minds. If you were to look hard enough, you might even be able to find a *career mentor* in your professional organization.

You may be asking, "Even if I *wanted* to join such an organization, how do I know one exists for people in my career?" The quickest way to find out is to consult *The Encyclopedia of Associations.* This exhaustive reference guide lists thousands of organizations in hundreds of different careers. The book can be found in most local libraries; consult yours.

Once you've compiled a list of the various organizations associated with your career, you'll probably want to narrow your selections to two or three. Many professional organizations boast their own web sites. If you're tooling around cyberspace, you might drop in on the organizations and check out their sites. If you'd like further information, perhaps regarding a chapter in your area, call or e-mail the national headquarters.

Bonus point: Did you know that membership in a professional organization looks good on a résumé? It suggests a commitment to one's craft, a willingness to get involved, and a capacity for networking—all traits that are highly regarded by employers.

BUT LEADERSHIP WRITES ITS OWN TICKET

If membership in a professional organization is your only intent, you will most likely still profit from your association with the group. If, on the other hand, you'd like to increase your profile in the industry, a professional organization is the perfect venue to do that.

All kinds of possibilities are available to you. You might volunteer to serve on a committee. You might answer questions or hand out brochures as part of the organization's exhibit at a conference or trade show. You might present a paper at an organization meeting. You might write an article for one of the organization's publications. In a few years, you might even consider running for office in the organization. Anything positive you can do to make yourself known throughout the group will only benefit you.

As is the case with subscriptions to industry magazines, many companies (or departments within the company) set aside a budget specifically for their employees' memberships in professional organizations. You'll need to ask your boss if your company does the same thing. If it does, what have you got to lose by joining? Take a chance, on your company's money, that you will enjoy and benefit from your association with a professional organization.

The Bible and Your Career Decision

THE BIBLE SAYS

God cares about your decisions.

The Bible says:
"You should say, 'If the Lord wants us to, we will live and carry out our plans' " (James 4:13, God's Word).

If, however, your company (or department) fails to recognize the many benefits of membership in a professional organization and denies your request for funds, you'll need to go to Plan B. Plan B, by the way, is to demonstrate to your boss how your membership in a professional organization will ultimately benefit the company. If you can list a few examples specific to your work, you'll have a good chance of changing your supervisor's mind.

Years from now when you reflect back on your career, it's possible that you will point to your membership in a professional organization as one of the keys to your success. Don't blow your opportunity to establish contact with people who, someday, may be able to help your career.

WHY KEEP LEARNING WHEN YOU'VE ALREADY GOT A JOB?

THE IMPORTANCE OF WORKSHOPS, SEMINARS, AND CONTINUING EDUCATION COURSES

Continuing education is a popular phrase in corporate circles today. It's no wonder, considering the world in which companies do business. Technology is being introduced at a mind-boggling rate. The time span between when a product is cutting edge and when it's obsolete is ridiculously short. New markets are constantly emerging while old ones are sliding into decline. Radical new methods, principles, ideologies, and ways of doing business are being implemented as we write this. How can anyone stay afloat in this sea of change? Only with a commitment to continuing education.

Less formal and structured than traditional university learning, continuing education exists in the form of workshops, seminars, and meetings. The focus of learning in each course is usually narrow and timely. Those workers who make a commitment to continuing education carve an important niche for themselves in corporate life. They become the office "answer people," the ones other people go to when questions arise. In short, they become vital members of the corporate team.

Let's take a closer look at how continuing education can benefit both you and your company.

THE BENEFITS TO YOURSELF

First and foremost, continuing education courses help you keep your skills sharp and your knowledge base broad. The more committed you are to continuing education, the more closely attuned you'll be to coming changes in your industry. Your ability to recognize emerging trends in their infancy will be a valuable tool to you and your company as you prepare to address those trends and make the necessary changes to accommodate them.

Workshops, seminars, and meetings are fertile breeding grounds for networking opportunities. You will find that some of your best industry contacts are made during breaks at continuing education events. It follows that those people who have a hunger for industry knowledge would seek out networking opportunities. And speaking on behalf of your career, you can never have enough contacts in your business network.

If you should ever decide to leave your company, your commitment to continuing education will look good on your résumé. Employers are looking for motivated workers, and nothing says motivation like an entire section of your résumé dedicated to recent workshops and seminars you've attended. Taking it one step further, keep this idea in the back of your head: the more continuing education classes you attend, the more comfortable you may become with the idea of actually *leading* a seminar or workshop. If you're uncomfortable with the prospect of speaking in front of crowds, you might write a paper for an industry publication. The point is, there will come a time when logical progression calls for you to become a teacher rather than merely a student. And we don't have to tell you what a leadership role would do for your career visibility.

THE BENEFITS TO YOUR COMPANY

We mentioned earlier how your company would benefit from your knowledge of emerging trends in the industry. The company may also benefit from the contacts you make at continuing education venues. *Synergy* is created when representatives from two different companies build a professional relationship based on mutual cooperation. Synergy is a good thing.

We also mentioned earlier that if you commit yourself to continuing education, to staying on top of issues and developments in your industry, you will become an "answer person" in your office, a fount of knowledge for all to enjoy. (Okay, maybe that's stretching it a bit.) But you *will* serve a valuable purpose in the office.

CATCH A CLUE

Who Picks Up the Bill?

Some companies include tuition and registration fees for workshops and seminars in their employee compensation packages. These corporations recognize the importance of continuing education both to their employees and to their organization.

Other companies, though, need to be convinced of continuing education's importance. If you work for such a company, you will need to educate your employers on the topic of, well ... education. To put it bluntly, you'll need to show them what's in it for them. Present a summary of the real benefits the company will see from your attendance. You will need to show something tangible and measurable. ("With the information I'll get from this software exhibition, I'll be able to choose the best program for our upcoming project.") Be truthful in your presentation, but tell your employers what they want to hear. Help them understand why you need to stay on top of industry trends and developments.

Remember, the only thing better than taking an active part in advancing your career through continuing education is doing it on the company's dollar.

A CODE TO LIVE BY

ETHICS IN THE WORKPLACE

What if someone asked you to write down your own personal code of ethics? Could you do it? Could you come up with a list of, say, six principles, ideals, or rules that govern your life and your business dealings? Six absolutes. Six statements of what you believe to be right and wrong.

Many people take a passive approach to right and wrong. They have no strong feelings about either one. As a result, when they're faced with a tempting situation—at work or anywhere—they have no strong principles to guide them. And in many instances they make regrettable decisions.

The business world is crawling with unscrupulous characters, people with plans and schemes to get ahead at any cost. Do you know the type? If not, you will. Someday they may use you in one of their plans. They may give you an opportunity for some serious cash or career recognition. All you'll have to do is "play along." And if you have no strong feelings about right or wrong, you might be tempted to do just that—at the risk of your reputation and your career.

Bad influences are just half of the story. If it were only "bad guys" you had to watch out for, corporate life wouldn't be such a minefield of ethical crises. After all, even the smoothest villains eventually show their true colors.

What you need to watch out for are the seemingly harmless everyday situations that catch you off guard or with your defenses down and cause you to consider things that are otherwise completely out of character for you. *Those* are the situations that can get you into trouble faster than anything.

We're not suggesting that writing a code of ethics is somehow going to magically protect you from the temptations of the business world. It will, however, give you a chance to think about the values that are closest to your heart and the principles that mean the most to you.

If you're still unsure about writing your own code of ethics, at least take a look at the ethical standards we've listed on the pages that follow. How many of them seem like sound principles to you, things you might include in your own code of ethics (if you had one)? Which ones seem a bit extreme to you? Which ones would never work in a business setting? Which ones are hopelessly outdated in today's high-tech, high-pressure culture?

ETHICAL BUSINESS: IT'S NOT AN OXYMORON

Here are six ethical statements, each of which has a specific application for the business sector. How many of them would you be willing to apply to your career?

1. I will maintain the highest standards of integrity in dealing with clients and coworkers.

Integrity is an all-encompassing word that suggests a moral basis beyond ethics, a deep-seated sense of right and wrong that governs every aspect of a person's life. Integrity is a proactive attribute, not a reactive one. For example, a person with ethics would recognize when he is facing a serious temptation and react appropriately. A person with integrity would avoid situations that might present a temptation. To put it another way, people with integrity do not put themselves in compromising positions.

2. I will deal fairly with everyone, giving due respect to the opinions of others.

Fairness is treating people in an appropriate manner, avoiding both favoritism and discrimination. Giving due respect to a person's opinion does not mean you have to agree with that opinion. It means that you show the person the courtesy of considering what he has to say. Of the six ethical statements, this one is probably the easiest to violate unwittingly. Think about it: How many people's opinions do you fail to respect every day? If you're like the rest of us, you'll find that the answer is "quite a few." If you recognize that you've failed to treat someone fairly or respect someone's opinion, apologize to that person and set the situation right at your earliest opportunity.

3. I will adhere to the highest standards of accuracy and truth.

Journalists, reporters, and tabloid editors, please step to the front for this presentation. Truth telling is fast becoming a lost art in corporate America. One of the best dodges for telling the truth is hiding behind legal mumbo-jumbo. The prevailing attitude is that it's not wrong unless you can be sued for it. The ethical position is that if it's not the truth, an accurate representation of the facts, it should not be presented as such. In an office setting that would include taking credit for someone else's work, inflating budgets, or making extravagant claims.

4. I will not knowingly spread false or misleading information.

Obviously, this covers gossip and lying. It could also apply to the questionable practice of quoting "unnamed sources." Take responsibility not only for your actions, but for your words. Don't say anything that you would be ashamed to take credit for later. If you find that you have unwittingly spread false information, act promptly to correct your mistake.

5. I will strictly maintain the secrets and privacy of my clients and co-workers.

If information is power, privileged information is ultimate power. In the course of your business dealings, you will likely become privileged to know some very personal information about your clients and perhaps even your co-workers. That privileged information can become a source of temptation under the right circumstances. You will likely face situations in which divulging that information could benefit you, perhaps by getting you in good with the boss or making you the center of attention at a party. This is a temptation that must be withstood at all costs. To reveal personal information about someone, under any circumstances, demonstrates a disturbing lack of self-control and untrustworthiness.

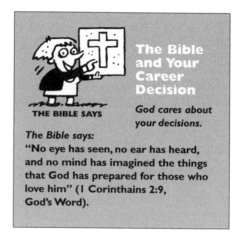

The Bible and Your Career Decision

God cares about your decisions.

THE BIBLE SAYS

The Bible says:
"No eye has seen, no ear has heard, and no mind has imagined the things that God has prepared for those who love him" (1 Corinthains 2:9, God's Word).

6. I will not intentionally damage the reputation of a client, co-worker, or competitor.

Think of the sleazy campaign ads you see every election year ("My opponent hasn't paid a dime of child support in the past nine years!" "My opponent allowed a child killer to be released from prison!") In the heat of battle, people tend to grab for anything that will damage their opponent. You may not have an "opponents" in your career, but chances are you have competitors, people vying with you for clients, promotions, or the respect of peers. And in the heat of competition, you may be tempted to question someone's reputation or repeat a damaging allegation. Don't do it, even if those tactics are being used against you. Stay above the fray. Compete hard, but fairly.

ETHICAL, NOT HEAVY-HANDED

To those of you who choose to draw up your own code of ethics: good for you! When questionable situations arise, you may find yourself pulling out your code for consultation. Don't allow yourself to dismiss your ethical standards. Ask yourself this question: "What's the worst that could happen to me if I follow my code of ethics?" Then ask, "What's the worst that could happen if I *ignore* my ethical standards?" One word of caution here: Just because you have a code of ethics doesn't mean that you need to impose your standards on your coworkers. Never be shy to share what you believe; but do it in a nonjudgmental way, or you may damage your relationship with your coworkers. Humility is the key. Remember, you're not Moses descending from Mount Sinai with the Ten Commandments inscribed in stone. You're a worker in corporate America just trying to build a career and do what's right (though not necessarily in that order).

LONG-DISTANCE OPPORTUNITIES

SHOULD YOU ACCEPT A TRANSFER?

There was a time, not too long ago, when this question was unthinkable. If you were fond of your job, of course you would accept a transfer. Declining a relocation offer, if not career suicide, was enough to knock you down several rungs of the corporate ladder. The reasoning was that if you weren't willing to move for the company, you weren't a "team player."

But things have changed. In today's job market, employees are much less likely to accept transfers than their counterparts were two decades ago. Employees today question whether relocation is necessary for career advancement. With jobs plentiful in today's worker-friendly corporate environment, there is much less pressure to accept a relocation assignment. Add to that a renewed emphasis on family and "quality of life," and you've got a generation of savvy workers unwilling to blindly go wherever management sends them. The result is a shift in power from employer to employee when it comes to filling jobs in "remote" outposts.

SWEETENING THE POT

In order to convince candidates to accept relocation assignments, many companies are starting to offer surprisingly enticing incentive packages. Often these packages include reimbursement for moving expenses, temporary living, house-hunting trips, real-estate services, and various other miscellaneous costs. Some prospective relocators have been lured with five-digit bonuses, country club memberships, and hefty salary raises.

Increasingly, employees are identifying dual-career concerns and aging parents as two of the major issues that complicate their relocation decisions. In response, companies are building into their transfer packages incentives that address these concerns. They are boosting the value of their packages by adding outplacement assistance for spouses, programs to help them write and distribute résumés in the new area, and financial support to help them maintain their skills. Some companies are even starting to offer assistance to help pay to move elderly parents and find caregivers or special facilities for them in the new location.

TAKING MATTERS INTO YOUR OWN HANDS

Of course, you can't expect your company to take complete responsibility for your well-being. Ultimately *you're* going to have to decide whether relocation is best for you. In order to make that decision, you'll need to do your homework.

The first thing you'll need to consider is what effect the move will have on the members of your family. Involve them intimately in the decision making. Give them as much information as you can. Explain what the move will mean for you professionally. Talk about what it will mean for them. Encourage an honest exchange of feelings, concerns, and excitement. Give serious thought to how devastating a move would be both to the family members who accompany you (spouse and kids) and those who are left behind (parents).

Second, you'll need to consider what effect the move will have on your career. Relocation traditionally has a reputation as a career booster. In some cases, though, it may have the opposite effect. Many professionals fear being "out of sight, out of mind." They believe that the farther they are from the company's hub of activity, the less likely superiors are to recognize the quality of their work. The consequence? Lost promotions.

Finally, you'll need to consider what effect the move will have on your pocketbook. The first thing to think about here is cost-of-living differences from city to city. Most people could guess that New York is a more expensive place to live than Little Rock, Arkansas. But how much more expensive? How much would a person have to earn in New York to equal her salary in Little Rock? (For your convenience, we've provided a simple chart and equation to help you calculate cost-of-living differences.)

When you consider the financial costs of moving, look at the obvious (your spouse's ability to find a job in your new locale) as well as the not-so-obvious (additional travel expenses for children in college returning home during school breaks). Find as many "hidden" relocation costs as you can and address them with your employer.

Relocation may be the key that unlocks the door to your career future. It may also be one of the most traumatic experiences of your life. Either way, your best course of action is to take your concerns to the Lord. Ask Him to guide your investigative process and give you and your family peace with the decision you make.

WHEN IS $50,000 NOT $50,000?

Here's a quick story problem for you: You're a mid-level executive in St. Louis. Your boss asks you to relocate to Boulder, Colorado. Though all of your moving costs will be taken care of, your salary of $50,000 will not change. How tempting is the offer? In order to truly judge it, you'll need to factor in the cost of living in both cities.

The fact is, some places are more expensive to live than others. What may seem like a decent salary in one region of the country might seem paltry in another. To accurately compare offers, you'll need to "level the playing field." And we've provided an equation to help you do just that. All you need is the following equation and the accompanying city-to-city index. Simply insert the index numbers provided for the two cities to determine the relative worth of your salary in each city.

Here's the Equation:

$$\frac{\text{(City \#1 index number) x (Salary)}}{\text{(City \#2 index number)}}$$

For the sake of practice, let's plug in the numbers from the story problem above. We want to find out the Boulder (City #1) equivalent of a $50,000 salary in St. Louis (City #2). The city-to-city index number for Boulder is 111.2. The index number for St. Louis is 97.7. So our equation will look like this:

$$\frac{111.2 \times 50,000}{97.7}$$

The sum of this equation is $56,908.90. So what?

Stick with us here; this is just slightly complicated. The Boulder equivalent of $50,000 in St. Louis is $56,908. So if you were to agree to transfer at your original salary, you'd actually be losing over $6,900 a year! It pays to investigate.

The City-to-City Index

The City-to-City Index is produced by the American Chamber of Commerce Researchers Association and is updated quarterly. The numbers reflect the cost of housing, transportation, health care, and consumer-items—everything except taxes. Cities not included on the list did not participate in the study.

Alabama
Birmingham 98.4
Huntsville 96.2
Mobile 95.6
Montgomery 100.9

Alaska
Anchorage 122.6
Fairbanks 128.2
Juneau 136.7

Arizona
Flagstaff 111.6
Phoenix 103.7
Scottsdale 104.9
Tucson 98.1
Yuma 102.5

Arkansas
Fayetteville 91.8
Little Rock 86.7

California
Bakersfield 101.1
Fresno 105.4
Los Angeles 115.9
Palm Springs 110.1
San Diego 120.2
San Francisco 152.5
Santa Rosa 137.9

Colorado
Boulder 111.2
Colorado Springs 104.0
Denver 104.7
Fort Collins 106.7
Pueblo 88.6

Connecticut
Hartford 125.4
New Haven 121.5

Delaware
Dover 101.8
Wilmington 108.8

District of Columbia
Washington D.C. 123.1

Florida
Daytona Beach 94.4
Jacksonville 94.4
Miami 106.1
Orlando 100.2
Pensacola 93.9
Sarasota 107.4
Tallahassee 99.9
Tampa 97.7
West Palm Beach 106.8

Georgia
Albany 92.6
Atlanta 100.6
Augusta 94.5

Hawaii
Honolulu 174.2

Idaho
Boise 102.6
Twin Falls 99.7

Illinois
Bloomington 102.0
Champaign/Urbana 102.4
Decatur 93.8
Peoria 102.1
Quad Cities 97.2
Rockford 102.5
Schaumburg 118.0
Springfield 97.8

Indiana
Bloomington 102.0
Evansville 96.8
Fort Wayne 91.1
Indianapolis 96.1
Muncie 98.4
South Bend 90.7

Iowa
Cedar Rapids 99.3
Des Moines 99.1
Dubuque 104.9

Kansas
Lawrence 100.2
Wichita 96.0

Kentucky
Lexington 96.7
Louisville 94.3

Louisiana
Baton Rouge 100.2
Lafayette 95.6
Lake Charles 95.6
Monroe 98.2
New Orleans 94.7
Shreveport 93.1

Maryland
Baltimore 98.2
Hagerstown 98.6

Massachusetts
Boston 139.9
Fitchburg 101.2
Framingham 129.4
Worcester 96.1

Michigan

Ann Arbor	113.5
Benton Harbor	103.9
Detroit	109.9
Grand Rapids	107.8
Holland	102.0
Lansing	107.1

Minnesota

Minneapolis	100.8
Rochester	100.4
St. Cloud	98.5
St. Paul	100.6

Mississippi

Gulfport	95.1
Jackson	91.4

Missouri

Columbia	92.8
Joplin	88.4
Kansas City	95.8
St. Joseph	93.0
St. Louis	97.7
Springfield	93.6

Montana

Billings	100.0
Bozeman	97.1
Great Falls	101.6
Helena	97.8
Missoula	101.3

Nebraska

Lincoln	89.9
Omaha	91.5

Nevada

Las Vegas	105.9
Reno	113.8

New Hampshire

Manchester	105.7

New Mexico

Albuquerque	102.6
Carlsbad	89.3
Las Cruces	99.9
Santa Fe	113.1

New York

Binghamton	95.8
Buffalo	97.8
Elmira	111.8
Nassau County	137.8
New York	228.5
Syracuse	102.7
Utica	102.5

North Carolina

Asheville	102.1
Charlotte	99.8
Fayetteville	98.1
Greenville	95.5

Raleigh-Durham 104.4
Winston-Salem 101.1

North Dakota
Bismarck 98.7

Ohio
Canton 95.4
Cincinnati 99.7
Cleveland 105.0
Columbus 102.7
Dayton 105.3
Toledo 100.3
Youngstown 96.5

Oklahoma
Oklahoma City 90.8
Tulsa 90.7

Oregon
Eugene 106.9
Portland 107.2

Pennsylvania
Allentown 103.0
Erie 105.5
Harrisburg 101.9
Lancaster 105.5
Philadelphia 123.0
Pittsburgh 108.4
Wilkes-Barre 99.6

Rhode Island
Providence 116.0

South Carolina
Charleston 96.6
Columbia 94.5
Greenville 99.8
Hilton Head Island 113.9
Myrtle Beach 97.7

South Dakota
Rapid City 100.3
Sioux Falls 95.4

Tennessee
Chattanooga 93.4
Knoxville 97.7
Memphis 93.1
Nashville 95.4

Texas
Abilene 93.2
Amarillo 90.8
Austin 99.4
Beaumont 96.6
Dallas 97.5
El Paso 95.4
Houston 93.9
Lubbock 91.4
San Antonio 88.2
Waco 90.5

Utah
Provo 100.1
Salt Lake City 105.1

Vermont
Barre/Montpelier 107.1
Burlington 112.3

Virginia
Fredericksburg 108.7
Hampton Roads 97.2
Richmond 101.9
Roanoke 93.3

Washington
Bellington 107.2
Seattle 113.9
Spokane 103.1

Tacoma 104.5
Yakima 105.2

West Virginia
Charleston 98.7
Martinsburg 88.3

Wisconsin
Appleton 97.1
Eau Claire 99.1
Green Bay 96.3
Madison 110.7
Milwaukee 107.6
Sheboygan 98.1

Wyoming
Cheyenne 94.4

HIGH PRESSURE PERFORMANCE

DEALING WITH STRESS

Stress kills. The word may not show up on any coroner's report or death certificate, but it kills just the same. Everything from heart attacks to suicides have been blamed on stress. While it may be difficult to avoid stress altogether, there are plenty of things you can do to lessen its effect on your life.

Do what you can to address it at work.

You may be surprised to find out that the biggest contributor to your stressful lifestyle is you—or more specifically—your work habits. With some key changes in the way you go about your job, you could reduce your stress load by 50 percent or more.

The first area you'll want to look at is time management. Is your stress the product of a never-ending game of "Beat the Clock"? Are you constantly feeling the pressure of deadlines and commitments? The simple solution is to guard against scheduling—or allowing others to schedule more activities every day than you can possibly finish. Okay, maybe it's not a simple solution, but it's a solution. A manageable workload is the key to mental health. That's not to say that you can rid yourself of tight schedules completely. There will be times when long hours and quick work are absolutely necessary. But those times should be the exception, not the rule.

Of course not all time management problems are created by outside sources like deadlines and impatient bosses. Some are the result of procrastination. If you're the type of person who prefers to put things off until the last minute, you're just asking for a juicy mouthful of stress. Practice good time management skills by tackling projects as soon as you get them. Resist the tendency to flirt with deadlines. Get your work done early whenever possible.

Finally, you may need to learn to delegate responsibilities to help you reduce your workload and stress level. If you have qualified people ready, willing, and able to help you with a project, it's foolish to try to do it on your own. Take advantage of all the resources available to you.

Seek help from your family and friends.

You may think it's noble to suffer alone and not trouble your friends and family members with your stress problems. Well, it's not noble, and you're not fooling anyone. Anybody who knows you well will recognize when you're stressed out. And they'll want to help. Denying the problem or sweeping it under a rug will only serve to distance you from the ones who care most about you.

Let your friends and family help you. Share with them what you're going through and how you're feeling. You don't have to monopolize every conversation with your misery, but also don't pull any punches. Be honest with them. Not only will they be able to give you emotional support, they may also find practical ways for relieving your stress in other areas—by keeping household affairs in order, for example. The point is, do not ignore your God-given support system by trying to shield your family and friends from the pressure you're under.

DEVELOP A STRESS-RELIEVING HOBBY

One New York stockbroker relieves his stress by flying fighter jets over the

Arizona desert. An Oregon credit officer bungee jumps off 180-foot bridges. A Colorado financial analyst practices feng shui, the ancient Chinese art of ordering one's environment to live in total harmony. A Minnesota accountant performs in jazz clubs. All of these people have found stress reduction in their hobbies. They claim that the focus their hobbies require allows them to forget about the pressures of the business world, even if it's for a short time.

You'll notice that "stress-relieving" and "relaxing" are not necessarily the same thing. A hobby that provides an adrenaline rush or physical exertion can be just as effective in relieving stress as needlepoint or reading. In other words, if you can find a hobby that reduces your stress by taking your mind off the pressures of work, go for it.

TAKE IT TO THE LORD

Do not neglect your time with the Lord. Maintain a regular prayer time as well as a regular Bible study, perhaps with a group of trusted friends. If you're not currently in one, a weekly Bible study/prayer group can do wonders for your stress. Being able to share with other believers exactly what you're going through can be quite therapeutic. Ask the Lord to help you relieve the harmful stress in your life. Similarly, ask Him to help you find ways to reduce the amount of pressure you face every day.

WHEN WORLDS COLLIDE

YOUR FAITH ON THE JOB

Let's call it dueling responsibilities. On the one hand, you have a responsibility to your employer to maintain the best possible working relationship with your fellow employees. On the other hand, as a Christian, you have a responsibility to share the good news of Christ with those who haven't heard it.

What does that mean for your relationship with your non-Christian coworkers? Can you share your faith with someone while at the same time maintaining a quality working rapport? Yes, but it's not easy. Here are some tips you might want to keep in mind.

AVOID AN US-VERSUS-THEM MENTALITY

The last thing you want to do is divide the office into two camps, Christian and non-Christian. You don't want one group to feel uncomfortable around the other. You certainly don't want an antagonistic spirit in your workplace.

If there are Christians in the office who are more zealous and confrontational than you are in their approach to witnessing, you may need to serve as a "buffer" between them and the objects of their evangelism. Likewise, if there are some outspoken critics of Christianity in the office, you may need to serve as a buffer between them and the objects of their ridicule. (You'll probably also need to maintain a thick hide yourself.)

Ultimately, the goal of any group of coworkers is to be productive as a team. Do what you can to foster teamwork in your place of employment. Don't allow people to focus on the differences that separate them; instead, call their attention to the similarities that bring you together.

TAKE GREAT CARE BEFORE CONFRONTING COWORKERS

If you're working day in and day out with the same group of people, circumstances are bound to arise that require confrontation. Maybe the subject will be foul language or lewd jokes in the office. Maybe it will be provocative attire. Maybe it will be questionable business practices or habits. Whatever the situation is, let's assume that you or your fellow Christians in the office find it offensive enough to warrant a confrontation.

Handle the situation with care.

You'll want to confront each person involved in a loving, concerned manner. Don't downplay your feelings—be honest. But resist any temptation to go holier-than-thou on the person. Don't quote Scripture to him. Don't make judgments. Just identify the problem and work with the person to come up with a solution that you can both live with.

WALK THE WALK AND LEAVE THE TALKING FOR LATER

When it comes to actually communicating your faith to others in the workplace, we suggest that you let two specific passages of Scripture guide you:

You are the light of the world. A city on a hill cannot be hidden. Neither do people light a lamp and put it under a bowl. Instead they put it on its stand, and it gives light to everyone in the house. In the same way, let your light shine before men, that they may see your good deeds and praise your Father in heaven (Matthew 5:14-16).

> But in your hearts set apart Christ as Lord. Always be prepared to give an answer to everyone who asks you to give the reason for the hope that you have. But do this with gentleness and respect, keeping a clear conscience, so that those who speak maliciously against your good behavior in Christ may be ashamed of their slander (1 Peter 3:15-16).

Everything about you—the way you work, the way you talk, the way you treat your boss, the way you treat your coworkers, the way you respond to adversity, the way you respond to others who are facing adversity—is a potential witness. If you let your "light" shine—that is, live your life consistently in a way that is pleasing to the Lord—people will notice. The curious among them will comment on it and perhaps even ask you about it. You've got a ready-made opportunity to talk about the hope you have, the salvation that Christ offers.

You don't have to wear a rainbow fright wig and a "John 3:16" sign to communicate the Gospel message. A simple lifestyle witness will do.

YOU, YOUR CAREER, AND YOUR COMPUTER

Job Resources on the Internet

If you're searching for a job or job-related advice, man, are you ever living in the right age! With just a few keystrokes and click or two of the mouse, you have access to an almost unimaginable amount of help. The Internet may be a career-minded person's best friend. The key, of course, is knowing where to look in the vast reaches of cyberspace.

Ideally the best way to find the information you seek is through a long, involved exploration in which you simply follow links that seem interesting to you. However, if you don't have the time or patience for such an exploration, we've compiled a list of sites that may be of interest to you.

For your convenience, we've divided the sights into four categories: positions available (job listings), job search helps (advice for job seekers), salary information, and career advice.

Happy hunting!

POSITIONS AVAILABLE

Want to check the job market for dental assistants in the Scranton, Pennsylvania, area? Chances are you'll find a web site with that information. Think of the Internet as a giant newspaper with millions of entries in its "help wanted" section. If you're willing to do the looking, you're likely to find a job opening with your name written all over it.

America's Job Bank (http://www.ajb.dni.us/)
Career Mosaic (http://www.careermosaic.com)
Career Path (http://www.careerpath.com)
Career Resource Center (http://www.careers.org)
Career Web (http://www.careerweb.com/jobs)
CoolWorks (http://www.coolworks.com)
E-Span (http://www.espan.com)
Job Center (http://www.jobcenter.com)
Monster Board (http://www.monster.com)
Online Career Center (http://www.occ.org)

JOB SEARCH HELPS

How important are your references in your job search? How long should you delay revealing your salary expectations in an interview? What should you write in a follow-up letter? These questions and thousands like them are answered online. If you have a question about your job search, you'll be able to find an expert on the Internet who can answer it—free of charge. Here are some sites to check out to find these experts.

Barron's (http://www.enews.com/magazines/barrons)
Business Week (http://www.enews.com/magazines/bw)
Economist (http://www.economist.com)
Forbes (http://www.forbes.com)
Inc. (http://www.enews.com/magazines/inc)
Journal of Commerce (http://www.enews.com/magazines/joc)

Los Angeles Times (http://www.latimes.com)
New York Times (http://www.nytimes.com)
U.S. Federal Government (http://www.lib.lsu.edu/gov/fedgov.html)
U.S. News and World Report (http://www.usnews.com)

SALARY INFORMATION

Want the latest numbers on how much your career is going to net you? With just a few clicks of your mouse button, those figures and more will be available to you. From aardvark trainer to zygote specialist, the Internet runs the spectrum of career salaries. (Of course, the more obscure your career choice, the harder you'll have to look for information. That means you, aardvark trainers and zygote specialists.) Obviously we can't list all of the sites dedicated to specific careers. Instead, we've selected sites that provide more general databases.

Abbott, Langer & Associates (http://www.abbott-langer.com/)
The Bureau of Labor Statistics (http://stats.bls.gov/)
California State University of Northridge (http://www.csu.edu)
JobSmart (http://www.jobsmart)
JobWeb (http://jobweb.org)
The Riley Guide (http://www.dbm.com/jobguide)
Wageweb (http://www.wageweb.com/)
The Wall Street Journal Interactive Edition (http://careers.wsj.com/)

CAREER ADVICE

From tips on getting along with your boss to advice on dealing with sexual harassment, you can find a lot of valuable career guidance in cyberspace-provided, of course, that you know where to look. *We* know where to look, and we've listed several sites that you should check out if you have a question about or problem with your career.

America's CareerInfoNet (http://www.acinet.org/resource/careers)
Career Magazine (http://www.careermag.com)
Career Resource Center (http://www.careers.org)
Employer & Employee (http://www.employer-employee.com)
Entrepreneurial Edge (http://www.edgeonline.com)
The Job Resource (http://www.thejobresource.com/career/)
Job Show (http://www.jobshow.com)
The Mining Co. (http://careerplanning.miningco.com/)
Taunee Besson's Career Advice FAQs (http://www.cweb.com/bessonfaqs)
Vault Reports (http://www.vaultreports.com/career/career.shtml)

SECTION 4
OVERVIEW OF JOBS

ACCOUNTANT

Accountant (e-koun'tent) n. One who keeps, audits, and inspects the financial records of individuals or businesses, and prepares financial and tax reports.

Accountants? Don't they just crunch numbers? Borrrriiiiiiing! Maybe so, but think about it in another light. Accounting is really a service provided to individuals and businesses.

Remember, Jesus said "render therefore unto Caesar the things that are Caesar's" (Matthew 22:21 KJV). He was acknowledging Caesar's right to assess and collect taxes, and, thus, the Christian's duty to pay them. In fact, two very important men in the Bible were tax collectors: Zaccheus and Matthew, who was one of Jesus' 12 disciples and the author of the book of Matthew (Matthew 9:9; Luke 19:2).

Well, it's no different today. We're still required by law to pay taxes; and who better to assist us in that duty than people like Zaccheus and Matthew, people who have the knowledge and expertise, namely certified accountants? Let's "crunch" the facts, shall we? Depending upon your interests, there are different specializations within accounting. Take a look.

WHAT THEY DO

Accountants help with:
- Bankruptcy investigation
- Designing accounting/data processing systems

- Employee compensation or health care benefits
- Budgeting/planning
- Cost/asset management
- Financial analysis
- Performance evaluation
- Banking
- Electronic data processing
- Engineering
- Health care
- Insurance
- Legal

On the Job

WOW!

People are always trying to find ways in which they can write off more of their taxes, so it came as no surprise to Walt Halloran, a certified public accountant, when one of his clients asked him this question. Walt looked across his desk at Jack Murphy, whose two-year-old daughter was sitting on his lap; and, without hesitating, he replied, "Have more children."

NOW, LET'S ANALYZE THE COST

Due to the exacting nature of accounting, CPAs must have a high level of technical competence, a sense of commitment to service, good communication and analytical skills, and the ability to work well with people.

To obtain the knowledge, skills and abilities necessary for CPA certification, many states now are requiring 150 semester hours of education. Colleges and universities that offer accounting programs determine the curriculum for pre-licensure education, which typically features a good balance of accounting, business, and general education.

Graduate level study further develops the communication, presentation, and interpersonal relations skills highly favored by accounting firms. And students who get a graduate education have a substantially higher rate of success on the Uniform CPA Examination.

Furthermore, those with master's degrees receive starting salaries that are approximately 10 to 20 percent higher than the starting salaries of those with only bachelor's degrees.

There is evidence that promotions to corporate managerial positions are increasingly going to individuals with master's degrees.

Finally, most universities and colleges require a PhD in order to teach accounting and other related courses.

For more information about the field of accounting, visit The American Institute of Certified Public Accountants (AICPA) Web site (http// www.aicpa.org.)

WIDE ANGLE

At-a-Glance

Accounting Licenses:
Accounting Practitioner (AP)
Accredited in Accountancy (AA)
Accredited Tax Advisor (ATA)
Accredited Tax Preparer (ATP)
Certified Information Systems Auditor (CISA)
Certified Internal Auditor (CIA)
Certified Management Accountant (CMA)
Certified Public Accountant (CPA)
Public Accountant (PA)
Registered Public Accountant (RPA)

Educational Requirements:
One-hundred and fifty semester hours in accounting related field.

Any examination required for specialized accounting license.

Earnings Based on Experience*:

Entry:	Roughly $22,000
I year:	$25,000–$39,400
I to 3 years:	$27,000–$46,600
Senior:	$34,300–$57,800
Manager:	$40,000–$81,900
Director:	$54,800–$109,800

*Salary variations reflect differences in size of firm, location, level of education, and professional credentials.

ADMINISTRATIVE ASSISTANT/ GENERAL OFFICE

WORKING GIRL

Remember the movie "Working Girl," where the ambitious but frustrated secretary (Melanie Griffith) takes advantage of her boss' (Sigourney Weaver) skiing accident to advance her own career? Well, who's to say that couldn't happen? Okay, so it's a bit far fetched. But, there is a lesson to be learned from that movie: Those with good ideas and dogged determination, not underhanded schemes, can succeed.

Besides, the chance of ever getting Harrison Ford (ahhhhhhh!!) as a "bonus prize" is slim to none.

WIDE ANGLE

At-a-Glance

Education: Most administrative assistant positions are entry level, requiring at least a high school diploma. More formal training, sometimes a college degree, is usually required for higher level executive assistant positions.

Outlook: This field is expected to have steady growth in the next decade.

Earnings:
Entry:	$16,710–$21,720
Experienced:	$25,300–$29,000+
Senior/Executive:	$35,000–$56,110+

THE FACTS

Do you typically associate administrative assistants as being the "low man on the totem pull?" Do you usually label them "gopher," meaning, go-for-this, go-for-that?

Well, let me assist you with the facts. Administrative assistants, yes, do the "grunt" work, as it's referred to, but where would most offices be without them? Nowhere, quite frankly. They are the backbone of every office; and without the backbone, well, we all know what happens: the skeletal structure collapses.

Would it surprise you to know that Jesus had help throughout His earthly ministry? Indeed, He did.

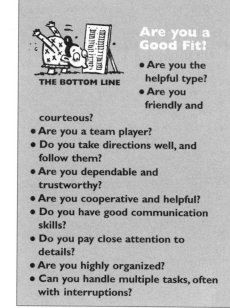

THE BOTTOM LINE

Are you a Good Fit?

- Are you the helpful type?
- Are you friendly and courteous?
- Are you a team player?
- Do you take directions well, and follow them?
- Are you dependable and trustworthy?
- Are you cooperative and helpful?
- Do you have good communication skills?
- Do you pay close attention to details?
- Are you highly organized?
- Can you handle multiple tasks, often with interruptions?

"Many women were there watching, from a distance. They had followed Jesus from Galilee to care for his needs" (Matthew 27:55). We don't exactly know what these women did, but quite possibly they helped with cooking Jesus' and the disciples' meals and took care of their belongings so Jesus was free to minister to the sick and needy.

Now most administrative assistants don't cook or clean in today's office environment, but their duties are nonetheless varied and diverse. Rather than performing a single specialized task, they change with the needs of the employer. One day they may file or type; another day enter data into a computer. It just depends on the needs of the day.

OTHER DUTIES MAY INCLUDE:

- Operate photocopiers, fax machines, other office equipment
- Prepare mailings
- Proofread copy
- Answer phones
- Deliver messages
- Sort checks
- Keep payroll records
- Take inventory
- Access information
- Organize files
- Make transparencies for presentations

THE EXECUTIVE . . . ASSISTANT, THAT IS

Larger corporations require more experienced professional assistants. Many top executives rely on their assistants to keep their business lives organized and running smoothly. An executive assistant, therefore, is given important responsibilities, such as:

- Maintaining financial or other records
- Verifying statistical reports for accuracy and completeness
- Handling and adjusting customer complaints
- Making travel arrangements
- Organizing company events
- Answering questions on departmental services and functions
- Helping prepare invoices or budgetary requests
- Overseeing and directing lower level assistants

It is recommended that assistants "gopher" higher education

Since most administrative assistant positions are entry level, only a high school diploma is necessary. However, to excel, most employers recommend that applicants have some training in word processing, computers, and basic office practices. Training of this nature can be obtained through most community and junior colleges, and postsecondary vocational schools. For the professional assistant, a college degree in Business Administration may be required.

Increasing use of computers and expanding office automation mean employers are looking for assistants who are highly versatile and have advanced computer skills. Those with advanced skills usually have a better chance at securing a job and advancing quickly to possibly an executive/supervisory position, and thus, up the pay scale.

ADVERTISING/MARKETING/ PUBLIC RELATIONS

ADVERTISING

Advertising is varied and diverse. It includes:

Account Services: Assesses the need for advertising and, in advertising agencies, maintains the accounts of clients.

Creative Services: Develops the subject matter and presentation of advertising.

Media services: Oversees planning groups that select the communication media (i.e. radio, television, newspapers, magazines, or outdoor signs) to disseminate the advertising.

Each of these departments is headed up by a manager or director

At-a-Glance

WIDE ANGLE

Education:
College graduates with degrees in journalism, public relations, advertising, or other communications-related fields.

Outlook:
This field is expected to have steady growth in the next decade.

Earnings:
Advertising
Entry:	$23,000–$29,000
Experienced:	$46,000–$97,000
Senior:	$105,000+

Marketing
Entry:	$23,000–$27,000
Experienced:	$46,000–$97,000
Senior:	$133,000+

Public Relations
Entry:	$15,000–$25,000
Experienced:	$34,000–$51,340
Senior:	$76,790–$150,000

who is responsible for the overseeing and delegation of each project to the satisfaction of the client.

MARKETING

Marketing managers develop the firm's detailed marketing strategy. With the help of subordinates, including product development managers and market research managers, they determine the demand for products and services offered by the firm and its competitors and identify potential consumers—for example, business firms, wholesalers, retailers, government, or the general public. Mass markets are further categorized according to various factors such as region, age, income, and lifestyle. Marketing managers develop pricing strategy with an eye towards maximizing the firm's share of the

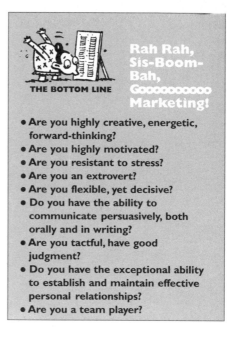

THE BOTTOM LINE

Rah Rah, Sis-Boom-Bah, Goooooooooo Marketing!

- Are you highly creative, energetic, forward-thinking?
- Are you highly motivated?
- Are you resistant to stress?
- Are you an extrovert?
- Are you flexible, yet decisive?
- Do you have the ability to communicate persuasively, both orally and in writing?
- Are you tactful, have good judgment?
- Do you have the exceptional ability to establish and maintain effective personal relationships?
- Are you a team player?

market and its profits while ensuring that the firm's customers are satisfied. In collaboration with sales, product development, and other managers, they monitor trends that indicate the need for new products and services and oversee product development. Marketing managers work with advertising and promotion managers to best promote the firm's products and services and to attract potential users.

PUBLIC RELATIONS

Public relations specialists are essentially advocates for their clients; advocates in the sense that they are in the business of building and maintaining their clients' identities, reputations, relationships, and, consequently, their profitability.

In a sense, John the Baptist "advertised" the coming of Christ, not by some huge media blitz (given there were no TVs, radios, or billboards then), but by the simple act of taking his message, as it were, "to the streets."

His project: "In the desert prepare the way for the LORD; make straight in the wilderness a highway for our God." (Isaiah 40:3).

His message (simple and direct, like an ad slogan): "Repent, for the kingdom of heave is near" (Matthew 3:2).

I don't mean to diminish the importance of John the Baptist's ministry whatsoever. On the contrary! I use it to illustrate a public relationist's need to get his client's message to its intended audience, simply and clearly, using whatever means necessary to do so.

These people specialists handle such organizational functions as media, community, consumer, and governmental relations; political campaigns; interest-group representation; conflict mediation; or employee and investor relations. However, public relations is not only "telling the organization's story." Understanding the attitudes and concerns of consumers, employees, and various other groups is also a vital part of the job. To improve communications, public relations specialists establish and maintain cooperative relationships with representatives of community, consumer, employee, and public interest groups and those in print and broadcast journalism.

Public relations specialists put together information that keeps the general public, interest groups, and stockholders aware of an organization's policies, activities, and accomplishments. Their work keeps management aware of public attitudes and concerns of the many groups and organizations with which it must deal.

Public relations specialists prepare press releases and contact people in the media who might print or broadcast their material. Many radio or television special reports, newspaper stories, and magazine articles start at the desks of public relations specialists. Sometimes the subject is an organization and its policies towards its employees or its role in the community. Often the subject is a public issue, such as health, nutrition, energy, or the environment.

Public relations specialists also arrange and conduct programs for contact between organization representatives and the public. For example, they set up speaking engagements and often prepare the speeches for company officials. These specialists represent employers at community projects; make film, slide, or other visual presentations at meetings and school assemblies; and plan conventions. In addition, they are responsible for preparing annual reports and writing proposals for various projects.

In government, public relations specialists—who may be called press secretaries, information officers, public affairs specialists, or communications specialists—keep the public informed about the activities of government agencies and officials. For example, public affairs specialists in the Department of Energy keep the public informed about the proposed lease of offshore land for oil exploration. A press secretary for a member of Congress keeps constituents aware of their elected representative's accomplishments.

In large organizations, the key public relations executive may develop overall plans and policies with other executives. In addition, public relations departments employ public relations specialists to write, do research, prepare materials, maintain contacts, and respond to inquiries.

People who handle publicity for an individual or who direct public relations for a small organization may deal with all aspects of the job. They contact people, plan and do research, and prepare material for distribution. They may also handle advertising or sales promotion work to support marketing.

AGRICULTURE/RANCHERS

What's the world's oldest profession? Farming. How so? Listen to this:

Let us make man in our image, in our likeness, and let them rule over the fish of the sea and the birds of the air, and over the livestock, over all the earth, and over all the creatures that move along the ground . . . I give you every seed-bearing plant on the face of the whole earth and every tree that has fruit with seed in it. They will be yours for food . . . And there was evening and there was morning—the sixth day (Genesis 1: 26,29, 31).

Can't get much older than that, now can we!

But, therein lies a problem: not everyone has the time, talent, or inclination to "rule over" every beast, tree, and plant of the earth. Thus, farming and ranching (or shepherding as it was in Biblical times) were created as man's response to fulfilling that command.

Today, however, farming is a more sophisticated enterprise, with high-tech equipment and machinery, state-of-the-art facilities, and million-dollar contracts with major food distributors. Today's farmers and farm managers direct the activities of one of the world's largest and most productive agricultural sectors. They produce not only most of our nation's food and fiber, but enough for other countries around the world.

TYPES OF FARMERS AND THEIR RESPONSIBILITIES

Crop Farmers: Grow grain, cotton, other fibers, fruits, and vegetables.

Livestock/Dairy Farmers: Raise and/or breed cattle, chickens, pigs/hogs, horses, sheep, ostrich, and llamas.

Horticultural Farmers: Produce ornamental and nursery plants, and greenhouse-grown fruits and vegetables.

Aquaculture Farmers: Raise fish and shellfish in marine, brackish, or fresh water for consumption or use in recreational fishing.

WIDE ANGLE

At-a-Glance

Education:
Hands-on experience and preferably a bachelor's degree in agriculture, or business with a concentration in agriculture. Agricultural programs, such as those sponsored by the National Future Farmers of America Organization or 4-H, are important sources of training as well. Agricultural scientists should have a bachelor's degree in animal or plant science.

Outlook:
This field will decline due to increasing productivity and consolidation in the highly efficient agricultural production industry.

Earnings:

Farmer:	Varies greatly year to year because of price fluctuations, weather, disease, etc.
Full-time Farm Manager:	$205–$760/week
Agricultural scientists:	$24,000–$65,500 (range includes specialties)
Rancher:	Varies greatly year to year because of price fluctuations, disease, etc.

FARM/RANCH MANAGERS

Farm managers manage the day-to-day activities to help maximize the financial returns of the farm or ranch. They typically are experienced professionals who are knowledgeable about farming or ranching and their operations. Depending on the size of the farm or ranch, the manager's responsibilities vary, ranging from managing the entire organization to overseeing just a single activity.

Agricultural Scientist

Agricultural scientists study farm crops and animals in order to develop ways of improving yield and quality. They also work on soil and water conservation, and research methods of converting raw agricultural commodities into attractive, healthy food products for consumers.

They can also
- Manage or administer research and development programs,
- Manage marketing or production operations, or
- Act as consultants to businesses, private clients, or the government.

Agricultural Science Specialties

Food Scientists: Usually employed in food processing industry, universities, or government agencies to help meet consumer demand for food products that are healthful, safe, palatable, and convenient. Must have knowledge of chemistry, microbiology, and other sciences to develop new or better ways of preserving, processing, packaging, storing, and delivering foods.

Plant Scientists: Study plants and their growth to help producers of food, feed, and fiber. It is helpful if they know breeding, physiology, management of crops, and genetic engineering.

Entomologists: Conduct research to develop new technologies to control/ eliminate pests in infested areas and prevent the spread of harmful pests to new areas. They also do research or engage in oversight activities aimed at halting the spread of insect-borne diseases.

Soil Scientists: Study the chemical, physical, biological, and mineralogical composition of soils as they relate to plant or crop growth. They study the responses of various soil types to fertilizers, tillage practices, and crop rotation.

Animal Scientists: Develop better, more efficient ways of producing/processing meat, poultry, eggs. Some animal scientists inspect and grade livestock food products, purchase livestock, or work in technical sales or marketing.

RANCHERS

The cattle industry is comprised of more than one million individual farms and ranches operating in all 50 states. Cattlemen form the largest part of the U.S. food and fiber industry, which is the largest segment of the U.S. economy. The total number of cattle on farms and ranches was 101.2 million in 1997. It is estimated that 45 percent of U.S. cattle ranches with more than one-hundred head have been in the same family for more than 50 years; 16 percent have been in the same family for more than 75 years.

Beef continues to be the most popular meat in America, with a per capita consumption in 1997 at 63.6 pounds, compared to 49.3 pounds for chicken and 45.7 pounds for pork. In 1997, U.S. cattlemen produced 25.4 billion pounds of beef with a total retail value of $50.6 billion. American consumers spent an average of $186.03 per person on beef in 1997. With all that beef being consumed, there's plenty of work for ranchers!

BANKING

"Go to the ant, O sluggard, observe her ways and be wise; which, having no chief, officer or ruler, prepares her food in the summer, and gathers her provision in the harvest" (Proverbs 6:6-8).

Okay, so what does this verse have to do with banks and banking? Plenty. This Scripture points out the necessity for laying aside money now in the event of troubles or shortages later.

This Scripture is even more poignant when you think about the fact that Social Security is expected to run out by the year 2029, which means that many of us will have to provide for our own retirement rather than rely on Uncle Sam as our predecessors did.

Sure, we're seeing more privatization plans, like 401K, being offered; but we can't rely solely on those either. That's where banks and those with banking expertise come into play. We need knowledgeable people to help us "[store] in summer" so that years later we can "gathers . . . in the harvest."

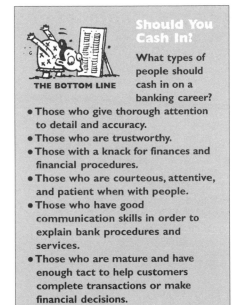

THE BOTTOM LINE

Should You Cash In?

What types of people should cash in on a banking career?

- **Those who give thorough attention to detail and accuracy.**
- **Those who are trustworthy.**
- **Those with a knack for finances and financial procedures.**
- **Those who are courteous, attentive, and patient when with people.**
- **Those who have good communication skills in order to explain bank procedures and services.**
- **Those who are mature and have enough tact to help customers complete transactions or make financial decisions.**

WIDE ANGLE

At-a-Glance

Education:

Bank Teller: High school education, with courses in mathematics, accounting, bookkeeping, economics, and public speaking.

New Accounts Clerk: High school diploma or equivalent; however, good interpersonal skills and familiarity or experience with computers are often more important to employers.

Loan Officer: Bachelor's degree in finance, economics, or related field. Most employers also prefer applicants who are familiar with computers and banking applications.

Financial Manager: A bachelor's degree in finance, accounting, economics, or business is the minimum requirement; however, a master's degree in business administration, economics, finance, or risk management is preferred.

Financial Services Sales Representaive: Bachelor's degree in business administration, with a specialization in finance; or liberal arts degree including courses in accounting, economics, and marketing.

Outlook:

Faster-than-average growth for most fields due to expanding population, growing economy, and increasing complexity of banking services. For financial managers, the future is uncertain due to continuing mergers and consolidations, which may eliminate these positions.

Earnings:

Bank Teller:	$11,900–$24,800
New Accounts Clerk:	$14,508–$23,244
Loan Officer:	$28,900–$48,000 (range includes specializations)
Financial Manager:	$62,000–$307,000
Financial Services Sales Rep:	$24,300–$73,500

COMMUNICATIONS

Writer (ri'ter) n. One who writes, especially as an occupation or profession; author.

Editor (ed~i-ter) n. 1. A person who edits, especially as an occupation. 2. One who writes editorials.

A writer is, simply, someone who communicates through the written word. It doesn't matter the venue either: letter, book, magazine, journal, newspaper, report, newsletter, broadcast, movie, advertisement, or Internet.

THE WRITE MOVES

Unlike in times past when anyone with a knack for verbosity could be a writer, the story's different today. Writing has become a highly specialized artform, often requiring a formal education. Most employers today prefer someone with a degree, either in communications, journalism, or English. And, some even require additional education or training and experience for

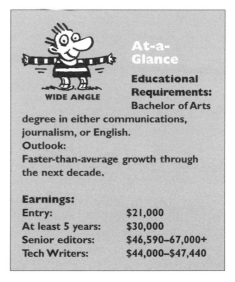

At-a-Glance

WIDE ANGLE

Educational Requirements: Bachelor of Arts degree in either communications, journalism, or English.

Outlook: Faster-than-average growth through the next decade.

Earnings:
Entry:	$21,000
At least 5 years:	$30,000
Senior editors:	$46,590–67,000+
Tech Writers:	$44,000–$47,440

WOW!

Trivia

Question:
What famous author gained fame when his story "The Celebrated Jumping Frog of Calaveras County" appeared in the *New York Saturday Press* on November 18, 1865?

Answer:
Samuel Clemens (a.k.a. Mark Twain). Clemens got his writing career started by working as a reporter for San Francisco's *The Morning Call* and by writing for local magazines.

Question:
What famous author had worked as a reporter for three parliamentary journals by the age of 22?

Answer:
Charles Dickens. He started writing for the *True Sun* at age 19, then later moved on to the *Mirror of Parliament* and *Morning Chronicle*, all by the age of 22 years. He published his first book *Pickwick Papers* at age 25.

specialty writing. Technical writing, for instance, is increasingly becoming the venue for many writers, which requires a degree and knowledge about a specialized field—engineering, business, or one of the sciences, for example.

While writing is communicating through the written word, writers and editors must be able to express ideas clearly and logically, and they should love to write. Also valuable are creativity, curiosity, a broad range of knowledge, self-motivation, and perseverance. The ability to concentrate amid confusion (i.e. newsrooms), and to work under pressure is essential. Familiarity with electronic publishing, graphics, and video production equipment is increasingly needed, and online publications require knowledge of computer software in order to combine text with graphics, audio, video, and 3-D animation.

Getting experience is highly recommended, beginning in high school and college. High school and college newspapers are great ways to gain experience. Also, magazines, newspapers, and broadcast stations hire interns and correspondents, which can help students build their portfolios and make contacts.

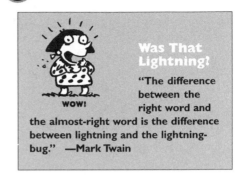

Was That Lightning?

"The difference between the right word and the almost-right word is the difference between lightning and the lightning-bug." —Mark Twain

Editors, on the other hand, play more of a supervisory role, which requires tact and the ability to guide and encourage others. They frequently write but more often review, rewrite, and edit writers' work. Their primary duties are to plan the content of the publication and to supervise its preparation. They decide what will appeal to readers, assign topics to reporters and writers, and oversee production.

Depending on the size of the organization, a single editor may do everything or oversee a staff of assistant editors who are responsible for particular subjects, such as fiction, local news, international news, or sports.

HOW DOES THE FUTURE LOOK?

Employment of writers and editors is expected to increase faster than the average for all occupations through the next few years. Employment of salaried writers and editors by newspapers, periodicals, book publishers, and nonprofit organizations is expected to increase with growing demand for their publications. Growth of advertising and public relations agencies should also be a source of new jobs. Demand for technical writers is expected to increase because of the continuing expansion of scientific and technical information, and the continued need to communicate it. Many job openings will also occur as experienced workers transfer to other occupations or leave the labor force. Turnover is relatively high in this occupation—many freelancers leave because they cannot earn enough money.

RELATED OCCUPATIONS

Authors: Develop original stories for books or magazines.

Advertisers: Write creative, attention-grabbing copy for ads to be placed in trade journals, newspapers, magazines, or other publication.

Columnists: Analyze news and write commentaries based on personal knowledge and experience. Columnists are able to take sides on issues, be subjective, and express their opinions while other newswriters must be objective and neutral.

Copy Writers: Write advertising copy for use by publication or broadcast media to promote the sale of goods and services.

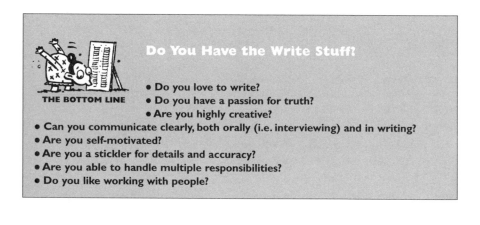

Do You Have the Write Stuff?

THE BOTTOM LINE

- **Do you love to write?**
- **Do you have a passion for truth?**
- **Are you highly creative?**
- **Can you communicate clearly, both orally (i.e. interviewing) and in writing?**
- **Are you self-motivated?**
- **Are you a stickler for details and accuracy?**
- **Are you able to handle multiple responsibilities?**
- **Do you like working with people?**

Established Writers: May work on a freelance basis selling their work to publishers, manufacturing firms, and public relations and advertising departments or agencies. They sometimes contract to complete specific assignments such as writing about a new product or technique.

Technical Writers: Make scientific and technical information easily understandable, prepare operating and maintenance manuals, catalogs, parts lists, assembly instructions, sales promotion materials, and project proposals. They also plan and edit technical reports and oversee preparation of illustrations, photographs, diagrams, and charts.

Reporters/Correspondents: Prepare news items for newspapers or news broadcasts based on information supplied by sources or wire services.

Public Relations: Gather information about a subject or organization to write a press release that is submitted to people in the media who might print or broadcast their material. Many radio or television special reports, newspaper stories, and magazine articles start at the desks of public relations specialists.

CONSTRUCTION

GENERAL MECHANICS

General maintenance mechanics are just that, general laborers. They have skills in many different areas.

- Repair/maintain machines, mechanical equipment, and buildings
- Work on plumbing, electrical, and air-conditioning and heating systems
- Build partitions
- Make plaster or drywall repairs
- Fix or paint roofs, windows, doors, floors, woodwork, and other parts of building structures
- Repair/maintain specialized equipment and machinery
- Troubleshoot and fix faulty computer systems and electrical switches
- Repair air-conditioning motors

WOW!

Strange but True

Dangling ten stories above the pavement, a construction worker hung precariously by a single cable. To all appearances, he seemed calm as he swung gently back and forth in the breeze.

A photographer from *The Daily Times* was busy clicking away with his camera, trying to get the best angle of the swaying construction worker.

When he had finished, he approached the construction manager, who was shaking his head in amazement.

"This ever happen before?" asked the photographer, his pen poised above his notebook.

"Yep. This ain't the first time this has happened to this guy. He has a knack for gettin' into scrapes," said the broad-shouldered, well-tanned manager.

"Really! Hmmm. Hey, I took his picture for the evening paper. Could I have his name?"

"Sure. It's John Klutz."

- Unclog drains
- Obtain supplies and repair parts from distributors or storerooms
- Use common hand and power tools, as well as specialized equipment and electronic test devices
- Replace or fix worn or broken parts
- Perform routine preventive maintenance to ensure that machines run smoothly, building systems operate efficiently, and the physical condition of the buildings does not deteriorate
- Inspect drives, motors, and belts; check fluid levels, replace filters

At-a-Glance

WIDE ANGLE

Education:
Most construction-related jobs require on-the-job training, with some prior apprenticeships. Most employers want laborers who are at least 18 years old and have a high school diploma. Only Construction & Building Inspectors and Construction Managers are required to have a bachelor's degree in construction or building science, or construction management, and have prior work experience as well.

Outlook:
Job opportunities for all fields should be steady to excellent because of rapid construction growth across the United States, especially in the urban areas, and because of high turnover rates.

Earnings:

General Maintenance Mechanic:	$334–$450/week
Construction Laborer:	$196–$478/week
Iron Worker:	$582–$1,074/week
Material Moving Operator:	$329–$806/week
Carpenter:	$267–$864/week
Drywaller/Lather:	$293–$891/week
Construction/Building Inspector:	$21,600–$55,800+
Construction Manager:	$28,060–$100,000+

CREATIVE EXPRESSIONS

"Beauty is in the eye of the beholder." And there are those that make beholding very pleasant and enjoyable, meaning those with the creative touch, like artists, actors, designers, and the such.

These unusually gifted people are able to communicate ideas, thoughts, and feelings through various methods, materials, and techniques, using their talents and training. Their repertoire can include paint brushes, pens, pencils, plaster, canvas, cameras, computers, fabrics, tap shoes, ballet slippers, their looks, their voices, and on and on.

AND ... ACTION!

Actors, directors, and producers express and create images based on a script in theaters, film, television, and radio. They "make the words come alive" for their audiences.

VOILA! IT IS MAGNIFICENT!

Artists are highly creative people and are often temperamental. While they may sell their works to stores, commercial art galleries, and museums, only the most successful

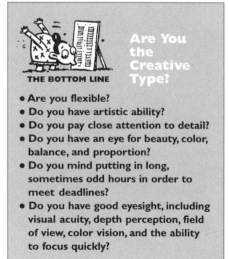

THE BOTTOM LINE

Are You the Creative Type?

- Are you flexible?
- Do you have artistic ability?
- Do you pay close attention to detail?
- Do you have an eye for beauty, color, balance, and proportion?
- Do you mind putting in long, sometimes odd hours in order to meet deadlines?
- Do you have good eyesight, including visual acuity, depth perception, field of view, color vision, and the ability to focus quickly?

artists are able to support themselves solely through sale of their works. Their subject matter and medium dictates the type of artist they are.

WIDE ANGLE

At-a-Glance

Education:

Actors, Directors, Producers: Formal dramatic training or acting experience is generally necessary either through theater, commercials, modeling, and acting groups.

Desktop Publishers: Four-year degree in graphic arts, or two-year associates degree coupled with on-the-job training.

Visual Artists: Bachelor's degree or other postsecondary training in art, design, or visual communications. Internships also provide excellent opportunities to develop and enhance talent. Knowledge and training in computer techniques are critical.

Photographers: College degree in photography, with courses in the specific field being photographed.

Cinematographers: Formal postsecondary training at colleges, photographic institutes, universities, or through on-the-job training.

Fashion Designers: Two-or four year degree in fashion design; knowledge of textiles, fabrics, ornamentation, and trends in the fashion world.

Furniture Designers: Some formal training; knowledge of trends in fashion and style, and methods and tools used in furniture production.

Floral Designers: High school diploma and on-the-job training; however, formal training is recommended for specialization and advancement.

Outlook:

Faster-than-average growth for most careers. Good competition and demand for printed materials is especially spurred by rising levels of personal income, increasing school enrollments, and higher levels of educational attainment.

Earnings:

Visual Artists:	$15,000–$43,000+
Photographers:	$14,500–$75,100+
Designers:	$27,000–$140,000+
TV/Movie Actors:	$29,068–$100,984+
Directors:	$43,250–$138,400+
Producers:	No set fee; gets percentage of show's earnings or ticket sales.

WOW!

Do You Know Who I Am?

I worked on and off as a carpenter and bit-part actor until I landed my first real acting job as a lead in *Star Wars* opposite Carrie Fisher. Who am I?

I was involved in a widely publicized "poor little rich girl" custody suit at age 10. Later, I achieved notoriety as a designer of housewares and fashion. Who am I?

At the age of 17, I left my factory janitorial job to help support my family. At the same time, I worked as the opening act for comedians Buddy Hackett and Rodney Dangerfield. Who am I?

At one point in my early life, before I studied art, I was an evangelist at Le Borinage. Who am I?

I was born in Cincinnati, OH. At the age of 13, I won a contest with a short feature film called *Escape to Nowhere*. Who am I?

I was commissioned to design a tomb for the pope, but constant interruptions and quarrels prohibited me from completing it. I was then ordered to decorate a church ceiling. I did so with great reluctance. Who am I?

One of my most noted accomplishments is that I developed zone exposure to get maximum tonal range from black-and-white film. Who am I?

My macabre cartoons of a ghoulish family were immortalized on television in the 1960s as *The Addams Family*.

Who am I?

Answers:

Harrison Ford	Steven Spielberg
Gloria Vanderbilt	Michelangelo
Jim Carey	Ansel Adams
Vincent van Gogh	Charles Samuel Addams

EDUCATION

Who among us can say we have never been influenced by a teacher? Not many. In fact, teachers can play pivotal roles in our lives, especially early on in our developmental years.

THE WONDER YEARS

Preschool Teachers (Child Care Workers): Nurture and teach preschool children in child care centers, nursery schools, preschools, public schools, and family child care homes. They play an important role in a child's development by caring for the child when the parents are at work or away for other reasons. They attend to children's basic needs.

Kindergarten and Elementary School Teachers: Play a vital role in the development of children. What children learn and experience during their early years can shape their views of themselves and the world, and affect later success or failure in school, work, and their personal lives. Kindergarten and elementary school teachers introduce children to numbers, language, science, and social studies. They use games, music, artwork, films, slides, computers, and other tools to teach basic skills.

Secondary School Teachers: Help students delve more deeply into subjects introduced in elementary school and expose them to more information about the world and themselves. Secondary school teachers specialize in a specific subject, such as English, Spanish, mathematics, history, or biology. They teach a variety of related courses—for example, American history, contemporary American problems, and world geography.

Special Education Teachers: Work with children and youth who have a variety of disabilities, including mental retardation, speech impairment, emotional problems, visual and hearing impairment, autism, or brain injury. Most special education teachers instruct students at the elementary, middle, and secondary school level.

College and University Professors: Teach and advise nearly 15 million full- and part-time college students and perform a significant part of our

WIDE ANGLE

At-a-Glance

Education:

Teachers: Public school teachers must have a bachelor's degree, complete an approved teacher education program, and be licensed.

Special Education Teacher: A bachelor's degree, completion of an approved teacher preparation program, and a license are required; many states require a master's degree.

College and University Professors: A PhD is generally required for full-time positions in four-year colleges and universities; in two-year institutions, master's degree holders may qualify.

Adult Education Teacher: A graduate degree may be required to teach nonvocational courses, whereas practical experience is often all that is needed to teach vocational courses.

Outlook:

Faster-than-average growth due to increasing population, especially in urban and suburban areas. Demand is particularly rising for adult education courses for career advancement, upgrading skills, and personal enrichment which will spur the need for adult education teachers.

Earnings:

Special Education Teacher:	$37,300
Adult Education Teacher:	$19,200–$60,000+
Public School Teacher:	$37,300
Private School Teacher:	$27,300
College and University Professors:	$30,800–$65,400
Education Administrator (Principal):	$56,500–$72,400

nation's research. Faculty generally are organized into departments based on subject or field.

Adult Vocational-Technical Education Teachers: Provide instruction for occupations that do not require a college degree, such as welder, dental hygienist, automated systems manager, x-ray technician, auto mechanic, and cosmetologist. Other instructors help people update their job skills or adapt to technological advances

Adult Remedial Education Teachers: Provide instruction in basic education courses for school dropouts or others who need to upgrade their skills to find a job.

Adult Continuing Education Teachers: Teach courses which students take for personal

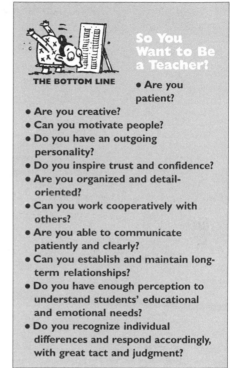

So You Want to Be a Teacher?

THE BOTTOM LINE

- Are you creative?
- Can you motivate people?
- Do you have an outgoing personality?
- Do you inspire trust and confidence?
- Are you organized and detail-oriented?
- Can you work cooperatively with others?
- Are you able to communicate patiently and clearly?
- Can you establish and maintain long-term relationships?
- Do you have enough perception to understand students' educational and emotional needs?
- Do you recognize individual differences and respond accordingly, with great tact and judgment?
- Are you patient?

enrichment, such as cooking, dancing, writing, exercise and physical fitness, photography, and finance. Some adult education teachers in junior or community colleges prepare students for a four-year degree program, teaching classes for credit that can be applied towards that degree.

Education Administrators (Principals): Provide direction, leadership, and day-to-day management of educational activities in schools, colleges and universities, businesses, correctional institutions, museums, and job training and community service organizations.

WOW!

The Blind Leading the Blind

One of the most awe-inspiring and heart-warming stories of a teacher and her pupil is that of Anne Sullivan and Helen Keller. Never before has a relationship between two women been so endearing, and critical to one's very survival.

It was Anne who taught the uncontrollable Helen about her world, a world in which she could not see or hear. But Anne introduced that world to Helen through the use of sign language. She spelled everything into Helen's hand. By doing this, Anne was equipping her pupil with the words and ideas she would need when she was ready to talk.

Anne helped Helen lead as normal a life as possible. Together, they would wander through fields, discussing whatever ideas came into Helen's mind. They pursued activities such as sailing and tobogganing.

As a result of Anne's constant attention and care, Helen became a more gentle, loving person. She also became an educated person, despite her disabilities. She learned to read and write in Braille; to read people's lips by pressing her fingertips against them and feeling the movement and vibrations; to even speak, which was a major achievement for someone who could not hear at all.

When Helen went to Perkins Institute for the Blind in Boston in 1888, Anne was right beside her. Helen proved to be a remarkable scholar and eventually graduated with honors from Radcliffe College in 1904. She had phenomenal powers of concentration and memory, as well as a dogged determination to succeed.

They spent many years on a world-wide lecture tour and a vaudeville tour. The two were inseparable, and they remained friends for 50 years, until Anne's death in 1936.

Helen relied a great deal on Anne. Without her faithful teacher, Helen would probably have remained trapped within an isolated and confused world.

And it's an even more remarkable story when you recall that Anne herself was nearly blind.

ENGINEERING

ENGINEERING A CAREER

Engineers, in general, apply the theories and principles of science and mathematics to research and develop economical solutions to practical technical problems. Their work is the link between scientific discoveries and commercial applications. Depending on their discipline, their job descriptions vary.

Aerospace Engineers: Design, develop, and test missile, spacecraft, and commercial and military aircraft, and supervise the manufacturing of these products. They are usually experts in aerodynamics, propulsion, thermodynamics, structures, celestial mechanics, acoustics, or guidance and control systems. They develop new technologies for use in commercial aviation, defense systems, and space exploration.

Industrial Engineers: Bridge the gap between management goals and operational performance. They try to determine the most effective ways for an organization to use the basic factors of production—people, machines, materials, information, and energy—to make or process a product or produce a service.

Mechanical Engineers: Plan and design tools, engines, machines, and other mechanical equipment. They design and develop power-producing machines such as internal combustion engines, steam and gas turbines, and jet and rocket engines. They also design and develop power-using machines such as refrigeration and air-conditioning equipment, robots, machine tools, materials handling systems, and industrial production equipment.

WIDE ANGLE

At-a-Glance

Education:
Engineers: A bachelor's degree in engineering is almost always required for beginning engineering jobs. Good employment opportunities are expected for new graduates. *Geological & Geophysicists:* A bachelor's degree in geology or geophysics is adequate for entry-level jobs; better jobs with good advancement potential usually require at least a master's degree; and a PhD degree is required for most research positions in colleges and universities, and for some research jobs in government.

Outlook:
Competitive pressures and advancing technology will force companies to improve and update product designs more frequently, and to work to optimize their manufacturing processes. Employers will rely on engineers to further increase productivity as they increase investments in plant and equipment to expand output of goods and services.

Earnings:

Engineers:	$34,400–$117,000
Aerospace:	$37,957
Chemical:	$42,817
Civil:	$33,119
Electrical:	$39,513
Industrial:	$38,026
Mechanical:	$38,113
Metallurgical:	$38,550
Mining:	$36,724
Nuclear:	$37,194
Petroleum:	$43,674
Geophysicist:	$59,700
Hydrologist:	$67,100
Oceanographers:	$62,700

Civil Engineers: Work in the oldest branch of engineering, designing and supervising the construction of roads, buildings, airports, tunnels, bridges, and water supply and sewage systems. Major specialties within civil engineering are structural, water resources, environmental, construction, transportation, and geotechnical engineering.

Chemical Engineers: Apply the principles of chemistry and engineering to solve problems involving the production or use of chemicals. Because the knowledge and duties of chemical engineers cut across many fields, they apply principles of chemistry, physics, mathematics, and mechanical and electrical engineering in their work.

Electrical and Electronics Engineers: Design, develop, test, and supervise the manufacture of electrical and electronic equipment, including power generating and transmission equipment used by electric utilities, and electric motors, machinery controls, and lighting and wiring in buildings, automobiles, and aircraft.

Metallurgical Engineers: Work in one of the three main branches of metallurgy: *Extractive Metallurgists* are concerned with removing metals from ores and refining and alloying them to obtain useful metal. *Physical Metallurgists* study the nature, structure, and physical properties of metals and their alloys, and methods of processing them into final products. *Mechanical Metallurgists* develop and improve metalworking processes such as casting, forging, rolling, and drawing.

Ceramic Engineers: Develop new ceramic materials and methods for making ceramic materials into useful products. Ceramic engineers work on products as diverse as glassware, semiconductors, automobile and aircraft engine components, fiber-optic phone lines, tile, and electric power line insulators.

Materials Engineers: Evaluate technical requirements and material specifications to develop materials that can be used, for example, to reduce the weight, but not the strength, of an object. Materials engineers also test and evaluate materials and develop new materials, such as the composite materials now being used in stealth aircraft.

Mining Engineers: Find, extract, and prepare coal, metals, and minerals for use by manufacturing industries and utilities. They design open pit and underground mines, supervise the construction of mine shafts and tunnels in underground operations, and devise methods for transporting minerals to processing plants.

Nuclear Engineers: Research and develop the processes, instruments, and systems used to derive benefits from nuclear energy and radiation. They design, develop, monitor, and operate nuclear power plants used to generate electricity and power Navy ships. They may work on the nuclear fuel or on fusion energy. Some specialize in the development of nuclear power sources for spacecraft; others develop industrial and medical uses for radioactive materials.

Petroleum Engineers: Search the world for underground reservoirs containing oil or natural gas. When one is discovered, petroleum engineers work with geologists and other specialists to understand the geologic formation and properties of the rock containing the reservoir, determine the drilling methods to be used, and monitor drilling and production operations. They design equipment and processes to achieve the maximum profitable recovery of oil and gas.

Geologists and Geophysicists (Geological or Geoscientists): Identify and examine rocks, study information collected by remote sensing instruments in satellites, conduct geological surveys, construct field maps, and use instruments to measure the Earth's gravity and magnetic field. They also analyze information collected through seismic studies, which involves bouncing energy waves off buried rock layers. Many geologists and geophysicists search for oil, natural gas, minerals, and groundwater.

FINANCE

Consider the ants. They are certainly the most industrious insects on Earth. They survive, literally, by planning, diligence, and labor.

So, what do ants have to do with us? Well, ants are used in the Bible (Proverbs 6:6; 30:25) as illustrations and rebukes to the lazy person who does not plan for the future and labor towards that end. Face it, to survive we need money, not necessarily lots of it, but we need it nonetheless if we are to pay our bills, buy food, pay our mortgages or rent, send our kids to college, etc. And especially so if we want to retire at a decent age and enjoy it.

Well, you're thinking, "But retirement's years, even decades, away for me." Maybe so, but saving, planning, and laboring for retirement needs to start right now! And to help us in at least the planning aspect are people who have the education, training, and resources. They're called securities sales representatives and Certified Financial Planners.

The Best Option

Securities sales representatives (also called stock brokers, registered representatives, and account executives) help those who cannot help themselves, with investing, that is. Given the education, training, and resources available, securities sales reps are most likely the best qualified to furnish information about the advantages and disadvantages of an investment based on an individual's or business' objectives, whether the investment is short- or long-term, or with a few hundred dollars or millions.

Planning for the Future

Certified Financial Planners (CFP) cover a greater spectrum of areas relating to investors' present security and future well-being than do securities sales representatives. While a broker can only cover investments, a CFP can cover everything from financial planning to insurance, risk management, tax computations and planning, employee benefits, government plans, and estate planning benefits and strategies.

Secure in Their Positions

Brokerage clerks perform many duties to facilitate the sale and purchase of stocks, bonds, commodities, and other kinds of investments. They produce

WIDE ANGLE

At-a-Glance

Education:

Brokerage Clerks: High school diploma. Clerks receive on-the-job training under the guidance of a supervisor or other senior worker.

Securities Sales Representatives: Bachelor's degree, preferably in finance, business, economics. Must meet state licensing requirements and be registered with their firm, according to National Association of Securities Dealers, Inc. (NASD).

Certified Financial Planners: Bachelor's degree and three years of financial planning-related experience, in addition to completing courses of study at a college or university that offers a financial planning curriculum, including those registered with the CFP Board. Must pass rigorous two-day CFP Certification Examination.

Outlook:

Faster-than-average growth as economic growth, rising personal incomes, and greater inherited wealth increase the funds available for investing.

Earnings:

Brokerage Clerks:	$27,300
Securities Sales Reps &	
Certified Financial Planners:	$18,100–$100,000+ (based on commissions)

the necessary records of all transactions that occur in their area of the business. Job titles depend upon the type of work performed.

Purchase-and-Sale Clerks: They match orders to buy with orders to sell, and they balance and verify stock trades by comparing the records of the selling firm to those of the buying firm.

Dividend Clerks: They ensure timely payments of stock or cash dividends to clients of a particular brokerage firm.

Transfer Clerks: They execute customer requests for changes to security registration and examine stock certificates for adherence to banking regulations.

Receive-and-Deliver Clerks: They facilitate the receipt and delivery of securities among firms and institutions.

Margin Clerks: They post accounts and monitor activity in customers' accounts to ensure that customers make their payments and stay within legal boundaries concerning stock purchases.

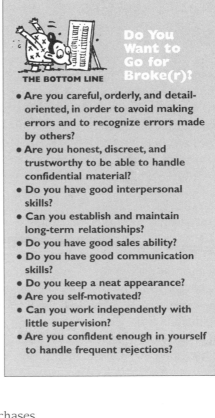

THE BOTTOM LINE

Do You Want to Go for Broke(r)?

- Are you careful, orderly, and detail-oriented, in order to avoid making errors and to recognize errors made by others?
- Are you honest, discreet, and trustworthy to be able to handle confidential material?
- Do you have good interpersonal skills?
- Can you establish and maintain long-term relationships?
- Do you have good sales ability?
- Do you have good communication skills?
- Do you keep a neat appearance?
- Are you self-motivated?
- Can you work independently with little supervision?
- Are you confident enough in yourself to handle frequent rejections?

HEALTH CARE

Chiropractors
Chiropractors diagnose and treat patients whose health problems are associated with the body's muscular, nervous, and skeletal systems, especially the spine. The chiropractic approach to health care is holistic, stressing the patient's overall well-being. They use natural, drugless, nonsurgical health treatments, and rely on the body's inherent recuperative abilities. They also recommend lifestyle changes—in eating, exercise, and sleeping habits, for example. When appropriate, chiropractors consult with and refer patients to other health practitioners.

Dentists
Dentists diagnose, prevent, and treat problems of the teeth and tissues of the mouth. They remove decay, fill cavities, examine x-rays, place protective plastic sealants on children's teeth, straighten teeth, and repair fractured teeth. They also perform corrective surgery of the gums and supporting bones to treat gum diseases. Dentists extract teeth and make molds and measurements for dentures to replace missing teeth. Dentists provide instruction in diet, brushing, flossing, the use of fluorides, and other aspects of dental care, as well. They also administer anesthetics and write prescriptions for antibiotics and other medications.

Dietitians & Nutritionists
Dietitians and nutritionists plan nutrition programs and supervise the preparation and serving of meals. They help prevent and treat illnesses by promoting healthy eating habits, scientifically evaluating clients' diets, and

WIDE ANGLE

At-a-Glance

Education:

Assistant Administrator: A bachelor's degrees in health administration.

Cardiovasular Technologist & Technician: Most are trained on the job, but more and more employers are looking for those with training in two- to four-year programs.

Chiropractor: Doctor of Chiropractic (DC) degree, obtained through four-year program, and licensure by National Board of Chiropractic Examiners.

Clinical Department Head: A degree in the appropriate field and work experience. A master's degree in health services administration usually is required to advance.

Dental Assistant: Most assistants learn their skills on the job, though many are trained in dental assisting programs offered by community and junior colleges, trade schools, and technical institutes.

Dental Hygienist: Graduate from accredited dental hygiene school and pass both a written and clinical examination administered by The American Dental Association.

Dentist: College degree, with two- to four-year postgraduate degree, either Doctor of Dental Surgery (DDS) or Doctor of Dental Medicine (DDM).

Dietitian, Nutritionist: A bachelor's degree, with a major in dietetics, foods and nutrition, food service systems management, or a related area.

Emergency Medical Technician: Certification in either EMT-Basic, EMT-Intermediate, and/or EMT-paramedic.

Health Services Administration: Master's degree in health services administration, long-term care administration, health sciences, public health, public administration, or business administration.

Home Health Aide: Federal law suggests, but does not require, at least 75 hours of classroom and practical training supervised by a registered nurse. Training and testing programs may be offered by the employing agency, but must meet the standards of the Health Care Financing Administration. Training programs vary depending upon state regulations.

Medical and Clinical Laboratory Technologist & Technician: Bachelor's degree in medical technology; master's degrees for specialized areas.

At-A-Glance ... Continued

Medical Assistants: Graduates of formal programs in medical assisting, with courses in anatomy, physiology, and medical terminology as well as typing, transcription, recordkeeping, accounting, and insurance processing.

Licensed Practical Nurse: Must pass state licensing examination after completing a state-approved practical nursing program. A high school diploma is usually required for entry, but some programs accept people without a diploma.

Nursing Service Administrator: A graduate degree in nursing or health services administration, plus state licensing certification.

Occupational Therapist: A bachelor's degree in occupational therapy.

Optometrist: A Doctor of Optometry (DO) degree from an accredited optometry school and passage of written and clinical state board examination for licensing.

Pharmacist: Either a five-year Bachelor of Science in Pharmacy, or six-year Doctor of Pharmacy (Pharm D) is required. Also internship under a licensed pharmacist and passage of state exam for licensing is required by most employers.

Physical Therapist: All states require physical therapists to pass a licensure exam after graduating from an accredited physical therapist educational program before they can practice.

Physician: Four years of undergraduate school; four years of medical school; and three to eight of internship and residency, depending on the specialty selected.

Physician Assistant: Two-year college program and some health care experience.

Podiatrist: A Doctor of Podiatric Medicine (DPM) degree, passage of state licensing exam. Continuing education for licensure renewal.

Psychologist: A Doctor of Psychology (PhD) is generally required for a licensed clinical or counseling psychologist. A bachelor's degree in psychology qualifies a person to assist psychologists and other professionals in community mental health centers, vocational rehabilitation offices, and correctional programs.

Recreational Therapist: A bachelor's degree in therapeutic recreation or in recreation with an option in therapeutic recreation.

Registered Nurses: Associate degree (ADN), diploma, or Bachelor of Science degree in nursing (BSN). Also, passage of national licensing examination to obtain nursing license and/or specialty licenses.

Respiratory Therapists: Most of the CAAHEP-accredited therapist programs last two years and lead to an associate degree. Some, however, are four-year bachelor's degree programs.

At-A-Glance ... Continued

Social Worker: A bachelor's degree is the minimum requirement for many entry-level jobs; however, a master's degree in social work (MSW) is generally required for advancement.

Speech/Language Pathologist and Audiologist: A master's degree or equivalent, plus 300–375 hours of supervised clinical experience, a passing score on a national examination, and nine months of postgraduate professional clinical experience.

Top Administrator (CEO): Graduate degree in health services administration, nursing administration, public health, or business administration.

Outlook:
Faster-than-average growth for all occupations as health services continue to expand and diversify.

Earnings:

Administrator (small group practice):	$56,000+
Administrator (large group practice):	$77,000+
Assistant Administrator:	$26,200–$40,000
Cardiovascular Technician:	$17,100–$33,600
Chiropractor:	$30,000–$170,000
Clinical Department Head:	$54,500–$97,000
Dentists:	$120,000–$175,000
Dental Assistant:	$11,024–$23,504
Dental Hygienist:	$39,468
Dietitian, Nutritionist:	$31,300–$43,374
Emergency Medical Technician:	$18,617–$32,483
Home Health Aide:	$10,920–$17,243
Licensed Practical Nurse:	$16,536–$34,996
Medical and Clinical Lab Technologists & Technicians:	$23,700–$37,900
Medical Assistant:	$16, 796–$27,976
Nurse Anesthetist:	$74,700–$90,300
Nurse Midwife:	$59,300–$75,700
Nurse Practitioner:	$54,200–$69,200
Nursing Home Administrator:	$42,100–$57,300

At-A-Glance ... Continued

Occupational Therapist:	$39,100–$46,100
Optometrist:	$57,000–$80,000+
Pharmacist:	$51,584–$61,735
Physical Therapist:	$30,004–67,288
Physician:	$115,000–$238,000+
Physician Assistant:	$49,100–$60,000
Podiatrist:	$44,662–$141,135
Psychologists:	$19,500–$62,120
Recreational Therapist:	$33,000–$42,000
Registered Nurse:	$21,580–$54,028
Respiratory Therapist:	$29,300–$35,000
Social Worker:	$32,900–$46,900
Speech/Language Patholigist & Audiologist:	$32,000–$55,000
Top Administrator (CEO):	$190,500+

suggesting diet modifications. Dietitians run food service systems for institutions such as hospitals and schools, promote sound eating habits through education, and conduct research.

Emergency Medical Technician
Emergency Medical Technicians (EMTs) give immediate care at accident sites and often transport the sick or injured to medical facilities. EMTs employ only those procedures for which they are certified.

Homemaker-Home Health Aides
Under the supervision of an RN, physical therapist, or social worker, home-maker-home health aides help elderly, disabled, and ill persons who live at home but need more extensive care than family or friends can provide, in assisting the home-bound patient.

Licensed Practical Nurses

Licensed Practical Nurses (LPNs) care for the sick, injured, convalescent, and disabled, under the direction of physicians and registered nurses. Most LPNs provide basic bedside care.

NURSES

By far the largest health care occupation, with over 1.9 million jobs, Registered Nurses (RNs) promote health, prevent disease, and help patients cope with illness. They are advocates and health educators for patients, families, and communities. It is the work setting and specialty which determine their day-to-day job duties.

Hospital Nurses: The largest group of nurses—provide bedside nursing care, carry out medical regimens, and supervise LPNs and aides. Hospital nurses usually are assigned to one area: surgery, maternity, pediatrics, emergency room, intensive care, treatment of cancer patients, or rotate among departments.

Office Nurses: Assist physicians in private practice, clinics, surgicenters, emergency medical centers, and health maintenance organizations (HMOs). They prepare patients for and assist with examinations, administer injections and medications, dress wounds and incisions, assist with minor surgery, maintain records, and perform routine laboratory and office work.

Home Health Nurses: Provide periodic services, prescribed by a physician, to patients at home. After assessing patients' home environments, they care for and instruct patients and their families. Home health nurses care for a broad range of patients, such as those recovering from illnesses and accidents, cancer, and childbirth. They must be able to work independently and may supervise home health aides.

Nursing Home Nurses: Manage nursing care for residents with conditions ranging from a fracture to Alzheimer's disease. Although they generally spend most of their time on administrative and supervisory tasks, RNs also assess residents' medical condition, develop treatment plans, supervise licensed practical nurses and nursing aides, and perform difficult procedures such as starting intravenous fluids. They also work in specialty-care departments, such as long-term rehabilitation units for strokes and head-injuries.

Public Health Nurses: Work in government and private agencies and clinics, schools, retirement communities, and other community settings to plan and implement programs in health education, disease prevention, nutrition, and child care. They arrange for immunizations, blood pressure testing, and other health screening. They also work with community leaders, teachers, parents, and physicians in community health education.

Occupational Health, or Industrial, Nurses: Provide nursing care at work sites to employees, customers, and others with minor injuries and illnesses. They provide emergency care, prepare accident reports, and arrange for further care if necessary. They also offer health counseling, assist with health examinations and inoculations, and assess work environments to identify potential health or safety problems.

Head Nurses (Nurse Supervisors): Direct nursing activities, which include planning work schedules and assigning duties to nurses and aides, providing or arranging for training, and visiting patients to observe nurses. They also insure that records are maintained and that equipment and supplies are ordered.

Nurse Practitioners: Diagnose/treat common acute illnesses and injuries. They can prescribe medications in most states.

Other advanced practice nurses include clinical nurse specialists, certified registered nurse anesthetists, and certified nurse-midwives.

OCCUPATIONAL THERAPISTS

Occupational therapists work with individuals who are mentally, physically, developmentally, or emotionally disabled, and help them to develop, recover, or maintain daily living and work skills. Their goal is to help clients have independent, productive, and satisfying lives.

WOW!

Who's Crazy?

"I was working in the psychicatric ward of a hospital in New York City. I entered a patient's room to do a series of tests. I was arranging my instruments and politely asked the patient, "Charles, how are you doing?"

"I'm fine. I'm watching the elephants," he replied.

He didn't look at me when he answered; he was staring blankly out the window. I wasn't surprised at his answer because you hear *many* strange comments when working in the psychiatric ward.

"Elephants? How many elephants do you see today?" I asked, trying to be polite (but I also knew there were *no* elephants outside his window).

"Six," he replied.

"I see. And what color are the elephants?" I asked.

"Gray." He said shortly and shot an angry look at me. "What color did you think they were?"

"Gray, I suppose," I answered.

I walked over to him and put the blood pressure cuff on his arm while glancing out the window. What I saw shocked me. There were six, gray, circus elephants walking down the middle of the street. Whether they were heading toward a circus or a parade I don't know. But what I do know was that there was someone in that room who wasn't as crazy as I thought!—*Frances, NYC*

OPTOMETRISTS

Over half the people in the United States wear corrective lenses. Optometrists examine people's eyes to diagnose vision problems and eye diseases.

Ophthalmologists

These are physicians who perform eye surgery, and diagnose and treat eye diseases and injuries. Like optometrists, they also examine eyes and prescribe eyeglasses and contact lenses.

Pharmacists

Pharmacists, for the most part, dispense drugs prescribed by physicians and other health practitioners and provide information to patients about medications and their use. They also advise physicians and other health practitioners on the selection, dosages, interactions, and side effects of medications. Pharmacists must understand the use, composition, and effects of drugs.

PHYSICAL THERAPISTS

Physical therapists provide services that help restore function, improve mobility, relieve pain, and prevent or limit permanent physical disabilities of patients suffering from injuries or disease. Their patients include accident victims and individuals with disabling conditions such as low back pain, arthritis, heart disease, fractures, head injuries, and cerebral palsy. While some physical therapists treat a wide range of ailments, others specialize.

- Pediatrics
- Geriatrics
- Orthopedics
- Sports medicine
- Neurology
- Cardiopulmonary physical therapy.

PHYSICIANS

Physicians serve a fundamental role in our society, affecting all our lives at one point or another. Generally speaking, they

- Diagnose illnesses,
- Prescribe/administer treatments,
- Examine patients,
- Obtain medical histories,
- Order, perform, and interpret diagnostic tests, and
- Counsel patients on diet, hygiene, and preventive health care.

Primary Care Physicians: Tend to see the same patients on a regular basis for preventive care and to treat a variety of ailments. When necessary, PCPs refer patients to specialists, who are experts in medical fields, such as obstetrics and gynecology, cardiology, psychiatry, or surgery.

General and Family Practitioners: Emphasize comprehensive health care for patients of all ages and for the family as a group.

General Internal Medicine: Provides care mainly for adults who have a wide range of problems associated with bodily organs.

General Pediatricians: Focus on children's health. When appropriate,

Psychologists: Psychologists study human behavior and the mind. They generally specialize in one of a number of different areas.

Health Psychologists: Promote good health through health maintenance counseling programs that are designed to help people achieve goals such as to stop smoking or lose weight.

Neuropsychologists: Study the relation between the brain and behavior. They often work in stroke and head injury programs.

Recreational Therapist: Recreational therapists provide treatment services and recreation activities to individuals with illnesses or disabling conditions, using a variety of techniques to treat or maintain the physical, mental, and emotional well-being of clients. Their focus is to help integrate people with disabilities into the community by helping them use community resources and recreational activities. They can work in park and recreation departments, school districts, hospitals, and clinics.

Respiratory Therapists: Respiratory therapists treat all types of patients, from premature infants whose lungs are not fully developed to elderly people whose lungs are diseased. They provide temporary relief to patients with chronic asthma or emphysema and emergency care for patients who suffered heart failure or a stroke, or are victims of drowning or shock. In home care, therapists teach patients and their families to use ventilators and other life-support systems. They visit several times a month to inspect and clean equipment and ensure its proper use and make emergency visits if equipment problems arise.

SPEECH/LANGUAGE PATHOLOGISTS AND AUDIOLOGISTS

Speech/language pathologists work with people who cannot make speech sounds, or make them clearly; those with speech rhythm and fluency problems; people with voice quality problems; those with problems understanding and producing language; and those with cognitive communication impairments.

HUMAN RESOURCES

THE HUMAN TOUCH

Attracting the most qualified candidates and matching them to jobs for which they are best suited is important, even crucial, for the success of most businesses. However, most businesses are just too large to permit direct contact between top management and employees. Enter human resource personnel. These highly trained and skilled workers are in the business of recruiting, interviewing, training, encouraging employees for the success of their company.

THE BOTTOM LINE

Is It a Fit?

Do You Possess the Right Resources for This Field?
Do you have strong leadership qualities?
Can you function effectively under pressure?
Can you cope with conflicting points of view?
Are you able to effectively handle the unexpected and unusual?
Do you have good communication skills, both orally and in writing?
Do you demonstrate integrity, fair-mindedness, and a persuasive, congenial personality?
Do you have the ability to encourage others and motivate them to work to the best of their abilities?
Do you have the tact to supervise people with various cultural backgrounds, levels of education, and experience?

WIDE ANGLE

At-A-Glance

Education:
Depending on the organization and position, employers look for college graduates who have degrees in either human resources, personnel administration, industrial and labor relations; or have a technical or business background.

Outlook:
Employment opportunities in human resources are competitive due to lots of qualified college graduates and experienced workers, despite large numbers of annual job openings that will stem from the need to replace workers who transfer to other jobs, retire, or stop working for other reasons, coupled with projected average employment growth.

Earnings:

Industrial/labor relations directors:	$106,100
Divisional human resources directors:	$91,300
Compensation and benefits directors:	$90,500
Employee/community relations directors:	$87,500
Training and organizational directors:	$86,600
Benefits directors:	$80,500
Plant/location human resources managers:	$64,400
Recruitment and interviewing managers:	$63,800
Compensation supervisors:	$53,400
Training generalists:	$49,900
Employment interviewing supervisors:	$42,800
Safety specialists:	$42,500
Job evaluation specialists:	$39,600
Employee assistance/employee counseling specialists:	$39,000
Human resources information systems specialists:	$38,800
Benefits specialists:	$38,300
E.E.O./affirmative action specialists:	$38,200
Training material development specialists:	$37,200
Employee services/employee recreation specialists:	$35,000

InfORMATIOn SERVICES/COMPUTERS

Have you noticed that America is fast becoming a bilingual country? No, I don't mean an international language (although it depends on how you look at it, I guess), but I'm referring to computer-eze. It's a language unto itself! Everyday, peoples' conversations are peppered with words like Web browser, service provider, gigabit, hyperlinks, e-mail, www._____.com. Some are so versed in computer-eze, they give the word "linquist" a whole new meaning.

Computer Programmers (Technicians): write, test, and maintain the detailed instructions—called "programs" or "software"—that list the steps computers must execute to perform their functions. Many technical innovations in programming have redefined the role of a programmer and elevated much of the programming work done today. Some programmers write specific programs by breaking down each step into a logical series of instructions the computer can follow, while others are involved in updating, repairing, modifying and expanding existing programs.

Applications Programmers: usually are oriented toward business, engineering, or science. They write software to handle specific jobs within an organization. They may also work alone to revise existing packaged software.

Systems Programmers: maintain/control the use of computer systems software. They make changes in the sets of instructions that determine how the network, workstations, and central processing unit of the

WIDE ANGLE

At-A-Glance

Education:

Computer Programmer: Bachelor of Arts or of Science in computer science, mathematics, or information systems is preferred. Some employers hire those with minimal education but experience and certification in computer programming.

Computer Systems Manager (Analyst): There is no universally accepted way to prepare for a job as a systems analyst. Many have degrees in computer or information science, computer information systems, or data processing and have experience as computer programmers. Bachelor's degree is usually required and a graduate degree is often preferred by employers.

Computer Operator: High school diploma or equivalent, with previous experience and familiarity with operating systems.

Outlook:

Faster-than-average growth for all industries, especially with the advent of the Internet and World Wide Web. Programmers especially desirable in data processing service firms, software houses, and computer consulting businesses.

Earnings:

Computer programmer:	$23,000-$60,000
Information systems:	$34,689
Systems analysis and design:	$36,261
Software design and development:	$39,190
Hardware design and development:	$41,237
Computer Systems Manager (Analyst):	$33,000 - $100,000+
Computer operator:	$13,800 - $41,400+

system handles the various jobs they have been given and how they communicate with peripheral equipment, such as terminals, printers, and disk drives. Because of their knowledge of the entire computer system, systems programmers often help applications programmers determine the source of problems that may occur with their programs. *Computer Scientists* generally design computers and software, develop information technologies, and develop and adapt principles for applying computers to new uses. Their jobs are distinguished by the higher level of theoretical expertise and innovation they apply to complex problems and the creation or application of new technology. They can work as theorists, researchers, or inventors; and be employed by academic institutions, the government, agencies, and organizations.

Computer Engineers work with the hardware and software aspects of systems design and development, emphasizing the building of proto-types. They generally apply science and math theories and principles to the design of hardware, software, networks, and processes to solve technical problems. They often work as part of a team that designs new computing devices or computer-related equipment, systems, or soft-ware.

Computer Hardware Engineers generally design, develop, test, and supervise the manufacture of computer hardware—for example, chips or device controllers.

Software Engineers (Software Developers) are involved in the design and development of software systems for control and automation of manu-facturing, business, and management processes. They also may design and develop both packaged and systems software or be involved in creating custom software applications for clients. These professionals also possess strong programming skills, but they are more concerned with analyzing and solving programming problems than with simply writing the code for the programs.

Computer Systems Managers direct and plan programming, computer operations, and data processing, and coordinate the development of computer hardware, systems design, and software. They analyze the computer and data information requirements of their organization and assign, schedule, and review the work of systems analysts, computer programmers, and computer operators. They determine personnel and computer hardware requirements, evaluate equipment options, and make purchasing decisions.

Computer Systems Analysts use their knowledge and skills to solve computer problems and to help an organization realize the maximum benefit from its investment in equipment, personnel, and business processes. They study business, scientific, or engineering data processing problems and design new solutions using computers. They may design entirely new systems or add a single new software application to harness more of a computer's power. Most systems analysts generally work with a specific type of system, depending on the type of organization they work for.

Telecommunications Specialists & Computer Security Specialists are growing specialty occupations reflective of the increasing emphasis on client-server applications, the growth of the Internet, the expansion of World Wide Web applications and Intranets, and the demand for more end-user support. Telecommunications specialists generally are involved with the interfacing of computer and communications equipment, while computer security specialists are responsible for planning, coordinating, and implementing an organizations' information security measures.

Computer Operators oversee the operation of computer hardware systems, ensuring that these machines are used as efficiently as possible. They may work with mainframes, minicomputers, or even networks of personal computers. Computer operators must anticipate problems and take preventive action as well as solve problems that occur during operations. Their specific duties vary with the size of the installation, the type of equipment used, and the policies of the employer.

Computer Technicians install equipment, do preventive maintenance, and correct problems. They work on mainframes, minis, and micros, peripheral equipment, and word processing systems. They also make cable and wiring connections when installing equipment, and work closely with electricians who install the wiring.

LAW ENFORCEMENT

PUBLIC SERVANTS

Police officers, detectives and special agents promote the safety and well being of our nation's citizens. Their duties vary widely depending on their title and job description. Did you know the Bible says this about them:

> Let every person be in subjection to the governing authorities ... those which exist are established by God. Therefore he who resists authority has opposed the ordinance of God; and they who have opposed will receive condemnation upon themselves. (Romans 13:1,2)

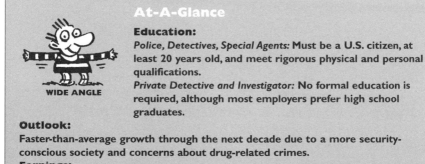

WIDE ANGLE

At-A-Glance

Education:
Police, Detectives, Special Agents: **Must be a U.S. citizen, at least 20 years old, and meet rigorous physical and personal qualifications.**
Private Detective and Investigator: **No formal education is required, although most employers prefer high school graduates.**

Outlook:
Faster-than-average growth through the next decade due to a more security-conscious society and concerns about drug-related crimes.

Earnings:

Police, Detectives, Special Agents:	**$22,500-$64,500**
Private Detectives and Investigator:	**$19,100-$67,700**

Police Officers generally patrol a designated area on the lookout for violators of the law. They also direct traffic at the scene of an accident, write up reports and maintain records. Some police officers specialize—microscopic analysis, firearms identification, handwriting and fingerprint identification—while others may work with special units—mounted and motorcycle patrol, harbor patrol, canine corps, special weapons and tactics, emergency response teams, or special task forces.

Detectives and Special Agents are plainclothes investigators who gather facts and collect evidence for criminal cases. They conduct interviews, examine records, observe the activities of suspects, and participate in raids or arrests.

Sheriffs and Deputy Sheriffs enforce the law on the county level. The sheriffs' department may also perform specialized duties such as serving legal documents or operating the jail.

State Police Officers (State Troopers or Highway Patrol Officers) patrol highways and enforce motor vehicle laws and regulations. They issue traffic citations to motorists, direct traffic, give first aid, assist stranded motorists, and call for emergency equipment. They also write reports that may be used to determine the cause of the accident. State police also are called upon to enforce criminal laws.

Federal Bureau of Investigation (FBI) Special Agents are the government's principal investigators, responsible for investigating violations of more than 260 statutes. Agents may conduct surveillance, monitor court-authorized wiretaps, examine business records to investigate white-collar crime, track the interstate movement of stolen property, collect evidence of espionage activities, or participate in sensitive undercover assignments.

Drug Enforcement Administration (DEA) Special Agents specialize in enforcement of drug laws and regulations. Agents may conduct complex criminal investigations, carry out surveillance of criminals, and infiltrate illicit drug organizations using undercover techniques.

U.S. Marshals and Deputy Marshals provide security for federal courts, including judges, witnesses, and prisoners, and apprehend fugitives.

U.S. Border Patrol Special Agents are responsible for protecting more than 8,000 miles of international land and water boundaries. Their primary mission is to detect, prevent and apprehend those found smuggling or entering undocumented aliens into the U.S.

Immigration and Naturalization Service (INS) Agents facilitate the entry of legal visitors and immigrants to the U.S. and detain and deport those arriving illegally.

Bureau of Alcohol, Tobacco, and Firearms Special Agents investigate violations of Federal firearms and explosives laws, as well as Federal alcohol and tobacco regulations.

Customs agents inspect cargo, collect appropriate duties or fees, and intercept contraband, while ensuring that all goods entering the United States comply with United States laws and regulations.

Internal Revenue Service Special Agents collect evidence against individuals and companies that are evading the payment of Federal taxes.

U.S. Secret Service Special Agents protect the president, vice president, and their immediate families, presidential candidates, ex-presidents, and foreign dignitaries visiting the United States Secret Service agents also investigate coun-

WOW!

All in a Day's Work

These are some actual, police-related headlines from newspapers across the country.

- "Police begin campaign to run down jaywalkers"
- "Drunk gets nine months in violin case"
- "Juvenile court to try shooting defendant"
- "Killer sentenced to die for second time in 10 years"
- "Drunken drivers paid $1000 in '84"
- "Stolen painting found by tree"
- "Victim tied, nude policeman testifies"
- "Police discover crack in Australia."

terfeiting, forgery of government checks or bonds, and fraudulent use of credit cards.

WHERE DO I START?

You can pick up an application packet from the fire and police department to which you want to apply. Expect to receive an intimidating stack of papers and overwhelming list of requirements. You'll learn very early in the process that only the most committed, eager and determined applicants get the jobs.

The application process is long and intense, sometimes taking as long as two years between the initial application and the time when a person is hired. You'll be evaluated according to your experience, physical and mental and psychological fitness, abilities and knowledge, and your personal integrity and character. Most departments conduct a detailed character investigation of every applicant, which can include checks of all credit references, school records, military records, interview of neighbors and previous employees, and a complete criminal background investigation. The testing process can include a written test, a physical agility test, a ride along for police officer applicants, an oral interview, a psychological exam, a polygraph, and a medical exam. Imagine the sense of personal satisfaction you'd feel if you made it through this process!

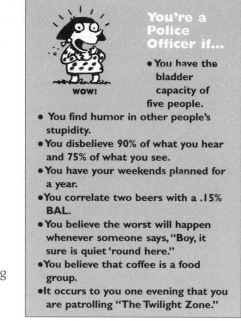

You're a Police Officer if...

WOW!

- You have the bladder capacity of five people.
- You find humor in other people's stupidity.
- You disbelieve 90% of what you hear and 75% of what you see.
- You have your weekends planned for a year.
- You correlate two beers with a .15% BAL.
- You believe the worst will happen whenever someone says, "Boy, it sure is quiet 'round here."
- You believe that coffee is a food group.
- It occurs to you one evening that you are patrolling "The Twilight Zone."

LEGAL

THE LAW LAID DOWN BY DIVINE DECREE

So, who likes the idea of lawyers and judges anyway? Would it surprise you to know that God endorses them? Indeed, our legal system grew out of a divine decree given during the lifetime of Moses. God decreed that justice be served among the Israelite people by having certain men be appointed as "judges and officials." (Deuteronomy 16:18-20 and Judges 2:16).

Our present-day lawyers and judges, similarly, act as our earthly advocates and judges; we should give them the honor and respect befitting their divinely-decreed positions.

Lawyers (Attorneys) act as both advocates and advisors. As advocates, they represent one of the parties in criminal and civil trials by presenting evidence in court supporting their client. As advisors, they counsel their clients as to their legal rights and obligations, and suggest particular courses of action in business and personal matters.

Judges' duties, on the other hand, vary according to the extent of their jurisdictions and powers.

General Trial Court Judges of the Federal and State court systems have jurisdiction over any case in their system. They generally try civil cases transcending the jurisdiction of lower courts, and all cases involving felony offenses.

Federal and State Appellate Court Judges have the power to overrule decisions made by trial court or administrative law judges if they determine that legal errors were made in a case, or if legal precedent does not support the judgment of the lower court.

Municipal Court Judge (County Court Judge, Magistrate, or Justice of the

---

At-A-Glance

WIDE ANGLE

Education:

Lawyer, Judge: Four-year college degree, followed by three years in law school. Passage of state bar exam.

Paralegal: Training can be obtained from either short-term paralegal certificate programs or four-year college degrees.

Legal secretary: Certification in either Accredited Legal Secretary (ALS), Professional Legal Secretary (PLS), or Civil Trial Legal Secretary (CTLS) depending on experience and specialization.

Court reporter: Two- or four-year program approved by the National Court Reporters Association (NCRA). Passage of state certification exam.

Stenographer: Skills are taught in high schools, vocational schools, community colleges, and proprietary business schools.

Outlook:

Faster-than-average growth due to growing population and the general level of business activities. Demand will also be spurred by growth of legal action in such areas as health care, intellectual property, international law, elder law, sexual harassment, Y2K law, and the environment.

Earnings:

Lawyer:	$30,000-$81,000+
Judge:	$68,900-$171,000 (highest paid being Chief Justice of U.S. Supreme Court)
Paralegal:	$29,300-$44,400
Court reporter:	$17,680-$56,160
Legal secretaries:	$19,700-$40,700

Peace) have limited jurisdiction. They typically handle traffic violations, misdemeanors, small claims cases, and pretrial hearings constitute the bulk of the work of these judges; however, some states allow them to handle cases involving domestic relations, probate, contracts, and other selected areas of the law.

Administrative Law Judges (Hearing Officers) are employed by government agencies to make determinations for administrative agencies, including a person's eligibility for Social Security benefits or worker's compensation, protection of the environment, enforcement of health and safety regulations, employment discrimination, and compliance with economic regulatory requirements.

MANUFACTURING AND PRODUCTION

PRECISELY THE POINT

We should never undervalue the work of manufacturers and those who labor in related fields. Without them, we would likely have to grind our own wheat for flour, make our own tables and chairs, and build our own houses and modes of transportation. Thankfully, in our day and age, there are many people who supply those parts for us.

Precision electrical and electronic equipment assemblers put together/modify prototypes or final assemblies of items such as missile control systems, radio or test equipment, computers, machine-tool numerical controls, radar, sonar, and appliances.

Precision electromechanical equipment assemblers prepare and test equipment or devices, construct, assemble, or rebuild engines and turbines, and office, agricultural, construction, oil field, rolling mill, textile, woodworking, paper, printing, and food wrapping machinery.

Precision aircraft assemblers put together and install parts of airplanes, space vehicles, or missiles, such as wings or landing gear.

Precision structural metal fitters align and fit structural metal parts according to detailed specifications prior to welding or riveting.

Welding machine operators set up and operate welding machines as specified by layouts, work orders, or blueprints. Operators must constantly monitor the machine to ensure that it produces the desired weld.

Flame cutters, instead of joining metals, use the heat from burning gases or an electric arc to cut and trim metal objects to specific dimensions. Cutters also dismantle large objects, such as ships, railroad cars, automobiles or aircraft. Some operate and monitor cutting machines similar to those used by welding machine operators.

WIDE ANGLE

At-A-Glance

Education:
Precision Assemblers: A high school diploma is preferred. Promotion comes from experience and on-the-job training. Some positions, such as electronics, may need more specialized training from a vocational or technical school.

Welders: Training for welders can range from a few weeks of school or on-the-job training for low skilled positions, to several years of combined schooling and on-the-job training for highly skilled jobs.

Tool and Die Maker: Four- or five-year formal apprenticeship, postsecondary programs, and/or on-the-job training.

Industrial Production Manager: A college degree in industrial engineering or business administration, preferably MBAs and undergraduate engineering degrees.

First-line Supervisor or Foreman/Forewoman: Usually promoted from among skilled employees who exemplify job knowledge, organizational skills, and leadership qualities.

Outlook:
Little to no growth in employment for precision assemblers and tool and die makers due to increasing automation and internationalization of production. However, there will be a significant demand for welders in many areas.

Earnings:

Precision Assemblers:	$11,180 - $30,004
Welders:	$14,456 - $41,964
Tool and Die Maker:	$24,960 - $60,320
Industrial Production Manager:	$60,000
First-line Supervisor:	$18,200 - $53,040

Toolmakers craft precision tools which are used to cut, shape, and form metal and other materials. They also produce jigs and fixtures (devices that hold metal while it is bored, stamped, or drilled) and gauges and other measuring devices.

Diemakers construct metal forms (dies) that are used to shape metal in stamping and forging operations. They also make metal molds for diecasting and for molding plastics, ceramics, and composite materials. In addition to designing and producing new tools and dies, these workers may also repair worn or damaged tools, dies, gauges, jigs, and fixtures.

Production and precision woodworkers still remain in demand in spite of the development of sophisticated composites. Production woodworkers can be found in primary industries, such as sawmills and plywood mills, as well as in secondary industries that manufacture furniture, kitchen cabinets, musical instruments, and other fabricated wood products.

Industrial production managers coordinate the resources and activities required to produce millions of goods every year in the United States. Their major functions include responsibility for production scheduling within budgetary limitations and time constraints, staffing, equipment, quality control, inventory control, and coordination of production activities with those of other departments.

First-line supervisor (or foreman/forewoman) oversees the responsibilities of blue-collar workers. A supervisor's primary task is to ensure that workers, equipment, and materials are used properly to maximize productivity.

OTHER CAREERS

We all have to work. But no matter what career path you choose, one thing holds true. "Whatever you do, do your work heartily, as for the Lord rather than for men; knowing that from the Lord you will receive the reward of the inheritance. It is the Lord Christ whom you serve" (Colossians 3:23).

Although we have earthly bosses, Christ, ultimately, is our Master. As His servants, we are to please Him in all that we do and say, including in our careers. And in pleasing Christ, we glorify Him; and in glorifying Him, we, in turn, are rewarded by a job well done, but ultimately and more significantly by the inheritance that awaits those who believe.

THE CLEAN CAREER

Janitors and Cleaners (Custodians, Executive Housekeepers, Maids) keep office buildings, hospitals, stores, apartment houses, hotels, and other types of buildings clean and in good condition.

A Career in Clean-Up
- Are you discreet?
- Are you particular about cleanliness?
- Are you dependable, trustworthy, and honest?
- Are you courteous and treat others fairly?
- Do you possess physical stamina?
- Do you like children, or the elderly (depending on employer)?

WIDE ANGLE

At-A-Glance

Education:

Janitors & Cleaners: No training is necessary, although high school shop courses are helpful for jobs involving repair work.

Private Household Workers: No training is necessary; however, special schools for butlers, nannies, and governesses teach household administration, early childhood education, nutrition, child care, and bookkeeping. These schools offer certifications—Certified Household Manager, Certified Professional Nanny, or Certified Professional Governess—and assist in job placement.

Vending Machine Repairers: On-the-job training.

Appliance & Power Tool Repairers: On-the-job training.

Electronic Equipment Repairer: One to two years of training, found through public post secondary vocational-technical schools, private vocational schools and technical institutes, junior and community colleges, and some high schools and correspondence schools.

Librarians: Bachelor's degree from any liberal arts program; master's degree in library science (MLS). Most employers prefer graduates of schools accredited by the American Library Association.

Funeral Directors: Must be 21 years old, have a high school diploma, and complete some college training in mortuary science and serve an apprenticeship. Must also pass state board licensing examination.

Barbers & Cosmetologists: Generally, a person must have graduated from a state-licensed barber or cosmetology school, pass a physical examination, and be at least 16 years old.

Veterinarians: A four-year degree (Doctor of Veterinary Medicine) from an accredited college of veterinary medicine and state license.

Forester & Forest Manager: Bachelor's degree in forestry is minimum educational requirement and state license. A bachelor's degree in range management or range science is the minimum educational requirement for range managers; graduate degrees generally are required for teaching and research positions.

Automotive Mechanics: At least a high school diploma. More formal training usually required for specializations.

Military: Enlisted members must enter a legal agreement called an enlistment contract, which usually involves a commitment to eight years of service. Depending on the terms of the contract, two to six years are spent on active duty, the balance in the reserves.

Earnings:

Janitors & cleaners:	$9,880-$29,640
Private household workers *(usually part-time work)*	
Cleaners & servants:	$11,600
Cooks:	$11,100
Child-care workers:	$10,50
Housekeepers & butlers:	$7,500
Vending machine repairers:	$18,012-$33,360
Appliance, power tool repairer:	$13,260-$48,308
Electronic equipment repairer:	$17,108-$50,908
Librarians:	$28,700-$58,400
Funeral director:	$21,775-$106,200
Barbers & cosmotologists:	$15,080-$25,480+
Veterinarians:	$29,900-$44,500
Foresters & forestry managers:	$19,500-$42,900
Soil conservationists:	$45,200
Rangeland managers:	$43,100
Forest products technologists:	$62,000
Automotive mechanics:	$13,000-$100,000
Military:	$46,800-$189,176

IT'S ALL IN THE REPAIR

Vending Machine Servicers (Route Drivers) visit coin-operated machines that dispense soft drinks, candy and snacks, and other items. They collect money from the machines, restock merchandise, and change labels to indicate new selections. They also keep the machines clean. Because many vending machines dispense food, these workers must comply with state and local public health and sanitation standards.

Appliance and Power Tool Repairers (Service Technicians) fix home appliances such as ovens, washers, dryers, refrigerators, freezers, room air conditioners, as well as power tools such as saws and drills. Some repairers only service small appliances; others specialize in major appliances.

Electronic Home Entertainment Equipment Repairers (Service Technicians) repair audio systems, televisions, disc players, recorders, public address systems, video cameras, video games, home security systems, microwave ovens, and electronic organs. Some repairers specialize in one kind of equipment; others repair many types.

SHHHHH! THE QUIET CAREER

The traditional concept of a library is being redefined, from a place to access paper records or books, to one which also houses the most advanced mediums, including CD-ROM, the Internet, virtual libraries, and remote access to a wide range of resources. Consequently, librarians are increasingly combining traditional duties with tasks involving quickly changing technology. There are a few aspects of library work:

User Services Librarians work with the public to help them find the information they need. This may involve analyzing users' needs to determine what information is appropriate; searching for, acquiring, and providing information; and showing users how to access information.

Technical Services Librarians acquire and prepare materials for use and may not deal directly with the public.

Administrative Services Librarians oversee the management and planning of libraries, negotiate contracts for services, materials, and equipment, supervise library employees, perform public relations and fundraising duties, prepare budgets, and direct activities to ensure that everything functions properly.

Library Technicians (Paraprofessionals) help librarians acquire, prepare, and organize material, and assist users in finding materials and information. As libraries increasingly use new technologies—such as CD-ROM, the Internet, virtual libraries, and automated databases—the duties of library technicians are expanding and evolving accordingly. They are assuming greater responsibilities, in some cases taking on tasks previously performed by librarians.

Library Assistants (Library Media Aides, Circulation Assistants) and Bookmobile Drivers keep library resources in order and make them readily available to a variety of users. They work under the direction of librarians, and in some cases, library technicians. Library assistants register patrons for library cards, and they enter and update patrons' records using computer databases.

(OMFORTERS IN TIMES OF LOSS

Since the earliest of times, most peoples have held funeral ceremonies. The dead have ritually been interred in pyramids, cremated on burning pyres, and sunk beneath the oceans' waves. Even today, funeral practices and rites vary greatly among various cultures and religions. To unburden themselves of arranging and directing the tasks of removing and interning the remains, grieving families turn to funeral directors.

Funeral Directors (Morticians, Undertakers) take great pride in their ability to provide efficient and appropriate services that give comfort to their customers, although this career does not appeal to everyone. They interview the family to learn what they desire with regard to the nature of the funeral, the clergy members or other persons who will officiate, and the final disposition of the remains. Together with the family, directors establish the location, dates and times of wakes, memorial services, and burials. They also send a hearse to carry the body to the funeral home or mortuary.

YOU LOOK MAAAAVALOUS!

Looking your best has never been easy. It requires the perfect hairstyle, exquisite nails, a neatly trimmed beard, or the proper make-up to accent your coloring. More and more, it also requires the services of barbers and cosmetologists.

Barbers cut, trim, shampoo, and style hair. Many people still go to them for just a haircut, but an increasing number seek more personalized hairstyling services, such as perms or coloring. In addition to these services, barbers may fit hairpieces, provide hair and scalp treatments, shave male customers, or give facial massages.

Cosmetologists (Beauticians, Hairstylists) primarily shampoo, cut, and style hair, but they also perform a number of other services. These workers may advise patrons on how to care for their hair, straighten or perm a customer's hair, or lighten or darken hair color. In addition, most cosmetologists are trained to give manicures, pedicures, and scalp and facial treatments; provide makeup analysis for women; and clean and style wigs and hairpieces.

NATURALLY, THIS WOOD BE A GREAT CAREER

The nation's forests are a rich natural resource, providing beauty and tranquillity, varied recreational areas, and wood for commercial use. Managing forests and woodlands requires many different kinds of workers.

Forestry Technicians compile data on the size, content, and condition of forest land tracts. They travel through sections of forest to gather basic information, such as species and population of trees, disease and insect damage, tree seedling mortality, and conditions that may cause fire danger. Forestry technicians also train and lead forest and conservation workers in seasonal activities, such as planting tree seedlings, putting out forest fires, and maintaining recreational facilities.

Forest Workers are less skilled workers who perform a variety of tasks to reforest and conserve timberlands and maintain forest facilities, such as roads and campsites. Some forest workers plant tree seedlings to reforest timberland areas. They also remove diseased or undesirable trees and spray trees with insecticides or herbicides to kill insects and to protect against disease.

Foresters manage forested lands for a variety of purposes. Those working in private industry may procure timber from private landowners, procuring trees for commercial purposes. Forestry consultants often act as agents for the forest owner, performing the above duties and negotiating timber sales with industrial procurement foresters.

Range Managers (Conservationists, Range Ecologists, Range Scientists) manage, improve, and protect the more than 1 billion acres of rangeland in the U.S. Rangelands contain many natural resources—grass and shrubs for animal grazing, wildlife habitats, water from vast watersheds, recreation facilities, and valuable mineral and energy resources.

Soil Conservationists provide technical assistance to farmers, ranchers, state and local governments, and others concerned with the conservation of soil, water, and related natural resources. They develop programs designed to get the most productive use of land without damaging it. Conservationists visit areas with erosion problems, find the source of the problem, and help landowners and managers develop management practices to combat it.

MR. FIX-IT

Anyone whose car, truck, boat, motorcycle, or farm equipment has broken down knows the importance of the mechanic's job. The ability to diagnose the source of the problem quickly and accurately—one of the mechanic's most valuable skills—requires good reasoning ability and a thorough knowledge of automobiles. Many mechanics consider diagnosing "hard to find" troubles one of their most challenging and satisfying duties. Career options include:

- Automotive Mechanics (Automotive Service Technicians)
- Automatic Transmission Mechanics
- Tune-up Mechanics
- Automotive Air-Conditioning Mechanics
- Front-End Mechanics
- Brake Repairers
- Automotive Body Repairers
- Diesel Mechanics (Diesel Technicians)

REAL ESTATE

"A man's home is his castle." We've all heard that saying, right? And how true it is! Just drive around some of the newer suburbs in a city near you and look at the luxurious, spacious homes being built. Houses have become a status symbol, a sign that we "have arrived."

WIDE ANGLE

At-A-Glance

Education:

Real Estate Agents, Brokers & Appraisers: All states require prospective agents to be a high school graduate, be at least 18 years old, and pass a written test. Most states require candidates for the general sales license to complete between 30 and 90 hours of classroom instruction, whereas those seeking the broker's license are required to complete between 60 and 90 hours of formal training in addition to a specified amount of experience in selling real estate (usually 1 to 3 years).

Property Manager: Most enter this occupation as an on-site manager of an apartment complex, condominium, or community association, or as an assistant manager at a large property management company. Opportunities should be best for persons with college degrees in business administration and related fields.

Outlook:

Slower-than-average growth through the next decade due to job competition and high turnover.

Earnings:

Real estate agents, brokers & appraisers:	$12,600-$75,400
Property managers:	$12,000-$60,700

But regardless of the size of the structure—whether it's a cozy bungalow or a 24-room mansion—buying real estate is one of the most important financial events in peoples' lives, not to mention one of the most complex as well. That's why people generally seek the help of real estate agents, brokers, appraisers, and property managers when trying to buy or sell, establish a price, or manage for their home or property.

Real Estate Agents have a thorough knowledge of the real estate market in their community. They know which neighborhoods will best fit their clients' needs and budgets. They are familiar with local zoning and tax laws, and know where to obtain financing. Agents also act as an intermediary in price negotiations between buyers and sellers. They are generally independent sales workers who provide their services to a licensed broker on a contract basis. In return, the broker pays the agent a portion of the commission earned from property sold through the firm, by the agent.

Real Estate Brokers are independent business people who, for a fee, sell real estate owned by others and rent and manage properties. In closing sales, brokers often provide buyers with information on loans to finance their purchase. They also arrange for title searches and for meetings between buyers and sellers when details of the transactions are agreed upon and the new owners take possession. Brokers also manage their own offices, advertise properties, and handle other business matters. Some combine other types of work, such as selling insurance or practicing law, with their real estate business.

Real Estate Appraisers often specialize in certain types of properties: homes, apartment or office buildings, shopping centers, commercial, industrial, or agricultural properties. Regardless of the property, their focus is the same: to investigate the quality of a structure or property, the overall condition, and its functional design to determine the assessed value of a property for tax purposes.

Property Managers, in general, oversee the performance of income-producing commercial and residential properties or manage the communal property and services of condominium and community associations. When owners of apartments, office buildings, retail, or industrial properties lack the time or expertise needed for the day-to-day management of their real estate investments, they often hire a property manager, either directly or by contracting with a property management company. Their responsibilities vary widely.

- Handle the financial operations of the property, seeing to it that mortgages, taxes, insurance premiums, payroll, and maintenance bills are paid on time;
- Supervise the preparation of financial statements and periodically report to the owners on the status of the property, occupancy rates, dates of lease expirations, and other matters;
- Negotiate contracts for janitorial, security, groundskeeping, trash removal, and other services;
- Solicit bids from several contractors and recommend to the owners which bid to accept;
- Monitor the performance of contractors;
- Investigate and resolve complaints from residents and tenants;
- Purchase supplies and equipment needed for the property;
- Make arrangements for any repairs that cannot be handled by regular maintenance staff.

Real Estate Asset Managers act as the property owners' agent and adviser for the property. They plan and direct the purchase, development, and disposition of real estate on behalf of businesses and investors. They are involved in long-term strategic financial planning rather than the day-to-day operations of the property. They periodically review their company's real estate holdings, identifying properties that are no longer commercially attractive. They then negotiate the sale or termination of the lease of properties selected for disposal.

RELIGIOUS

GETTING PAID FOR DOING GOD'S WORK

Pastors, Directors of Christian Education, Church Music Directors, Student Ministries Pastors, Children's Ministries Leaders, Religious Educators, Church-Planters, Missionaries: All of these people get paid for doing God's work.

Sounds pretty good, doesn't it? What committed Christian wouldn't love to receive a regular paycheck for helping out in their church? Well, a career in ministry can be one of the most demanding and life-consuming jobs you can have. But it can also be the most fulfilling and rewarding line of work you can choose. And the rewards last longer than your paycheck, your investment can last for an eternity!

THE INSIDE SCOOP

What it is really like to be on staff at a church or Christian organization? What is missionary life like? Do you have to be a "Jack of All Trades" to be involved in Christian service? Although everyone's experience is different, most Christian workers find themselves doing many of the same things on the job. If you get involved in religious work, here are a few things you'll find yourself doing:

- Recruiting and training leaders
- Teaching

- Mentoring
- Sharing your faith
- Counseling
- Administrative work
- Public speaking

Besides these basics, you'll end up doing countless other tasks that are not listed in your job description:
- fixing the church's leaky faucets,
- accepting the criticism of well-meaning members after every Sunday service,
- serving as the victim in the dunk tank at the annual church carnival,
- changing diapers in the church nursery when some of the scheduled volunteers call in sick,
- helping a parishioner move to a new house across town,
- baking 300 of your famous lemon bars for the youth group's bake sale,
- chairing the building committee because no one else will do it, and
- visiting the elderly aunt of one of your members who needs to tell some- one about her aches and pains.

You can see why God calls a select few to His service! Not many have the flexibility, humility, relational skills, toughness and tenderness necessary for full-time ministry.

DON'T DO IT FOR THE MONEY

The pay scale for full-time Christian workers varies greatly. Some pastors of rural churches need second jobs to support their families, while senior pastors of large, urban churches can be very well-paid.

Most missionaries depend on the financial contributions of their supporters so their monthly income can vary. Other missionaries are given a regular income from their denomination based on the cost of living in the country they serve. According to American standards, most missionary's salaries are below poverty level.

Whatever career you choose to pursue, money cannot be the motivating force. You will only find true fulfillment in your job if your ultimate goal is to honor God with your work.

IS IT WORTH THE SACRIFICE?

A career in full-time ministry requires personal sacrifice. No matter what area of ministry you choose, whether it is in the local church or overseas, you may have to sacrifice your financial security, your reputation or some of your relationships, a level of personal comfort, your aspirations or maybe some of your dreams for the future. But God's Word promises that anyone who gives up personal gain for eternal things will be rewarded. In Matthew 19:29, Jesus told his followers, "Everyone who has left houses or brothers or sisters or father or mother or children or fields for my sake will receive a hundred times as much and will inherit eternal life."

SHOW ME THE JOBS

The classified ads in your local newspaper is a good place to start but if you don't find much there, try these other options.

Check out your college career development office: You can visit their office in person or log on to their web site (call the office for the web site address and password). Ask for or look up their "career-oriented" positions in the category of "church and ministry." Most offices also publish a job opportunities bulletin to which you can subscribe.

Browse through the magazine section of your local Christian bookstore: Church leadership magazines such as *Vital Ministry* for pastors, *Group* magazine for youth leaders and *Children's Ministry* for Christian education leaders have a "Resource Directory" section that lists ministry positions available across the country.

Call and/or visit the web sites of reputable Christian organizations and mission agencies to see what opportunities they have available.

WHAT YOU NEED TO GET THE JOB

The qualifications for a religious job in America vary as much as the positions available. Most senior level positions require at least a bachelor's degree, and sometimes a master's, as well as several years of experience. On the other extreme, some churches advertise they are looking for "someone who loves Jesus and wants to learn how to be a leader."

If you are interested in cross-cultural ministry or missions work, you can choose from dozens of reputable sending organizations, all of which list different requirements. Some agencies require candidates to have a bachelor's degree and at least 2 years of ministry experience in the United States before they will consider sending them overseas. Many agencies require missionaries to raise their own financial support before they go to the field. Others provide monthly support for their missionaries but require them to assist in the fund-raising process by visiting churches and other donors.

RETAIL

Have you ever heard that old adage "Never judge a book by it's cover?" That may be true of books, but not with retail. Most customers, believe it or not, form their impressions of a store by evaluating its sales force. You may say that's pretty shallow, but it's true! Consumers spend millions of dollars every day on merchandise. They want to know they're getting the best bargain for their bucks. Who better to tell them and assist them in that decision-making process? Retail workers, that's who, from the salesperson on the floor right on up to store management.

It's no wonder, then, that retail establishments put a lot of stock (no pun intended) in their employees. Retail is big business, and first impressions do count.

BEHIND THE SCENES

Retail Supervisors and Managers (Department Managers) provide day-to-day oversight of individual departments, whether it's a department store or automotive dealership. Their overall responsibilities include:
- Establish and implement policies, goals, objectives, and procedures;
- Coordinate activities with other managers;
- Strive for smooth operations;
- Supervise employees;
- Clean and organize shelves, displays, and inventory;
- Inspect merchandise to ensure that none is outdated;
- Review inventory and sales records;

- Develop merchandising techniques;
- Coordinate sales promotions;
- Greet/assist customers;
- Promote sales and good public relations.

Buyers buy goods for the purpose of resale. They determine which commodities are best, choose the suppliers, negotiate prices, and award con-

---

At-A-Glance

Education:

Retail Sales Supervisors & Managers: **An associate or bachelor's degree in liberal arts, social science, business, or management is preferred, but not required. Knowledge of management principles and practices are essential.**

Buyers: **Experience and familiarity in merchandising, and wholesaling and retailing practices.**

Retail Sales Worker: **A high school diploma or equivalent is preferred.**

Fashion Designer: **A two- or four-year degree is usually required. Knowledgeable in textiles, fabrics, and ornamentation, as well as trends in the fashion world highly recommended.**

Outlook:

Growth in this industry will be restrained as retail companies place more emphasis on sales staff employment levels and increase the number of responsibilities their retail sales worker supervisors and managers have. Some companies have begun requiring their sales staff to report directly to upper management personnel, bypassing the department-level manager.

Earnings:

Retail Sales Supervisors & Managers:	**$12,400-$54,400**
Buyers:	**$18,400-$51,110**
Retail Sales Workers:	**$13,700-$30,836**
Fashion Designers:	**$19,760-$140,000+**

WIDE ANGLE

tracts to ensure the correct amount is received and at the appropriate time.

UP CLOSE AND IN PERSON

Retail Sales Workers are the most visible workers, therefore, being the most
courteous and helpful. They assist customers in finding what they're
looking for and try to interest them in the merchandise, whether it's
shoes, computer equipment, or automobiles. They must know their
company's product or service inside and out in order to adequately
describe the features or benefits, demonstrate its use, or show various
models and colors. Sales workers may also handle returns and exchanges of merchandise, perform gift wrapping services, stock shelves
or racks, arrange for mailing or delivery of purchases, mark price tags,
take inventory, and prepare displays.

Cashiers are in similar high visibility positions. They can be found in just
about every retail setting, from supermarkets to theaters. Their primary
function is to register the sale of merchandise. Cashiers can also handle
returns and exchanges and must ensure that merchandise is in good
condition and determine where and when it was purchased and what
type of payment was used.

TRANSPORTATION

UP, UP, AND AWAY!

Flying has become one of the most popular modes of transportation with millions of flights daily cross-country and increasingly overseas on business and pleasure. We rely on highly trained professionals to get us where we want to go quickly, comfortably, and safely. And we're willing to pay the price of doing so. Careers include: commercial airline pilots, helicopter pilots, pilot instructors, pilot examiners, airline attendants, and air traffic controllers (terminal controllers).

ALL ABOARD

Railroad transportation is one of the centerpieces of the U.S.'s transportation network, delivering thousands of travelers and millions of tons of freight to destinations throughout the nation. Subways and streetcars, on the other hand, provide passenger service within a single metropolitan area. Careers include: locomotive engineers, freight train conductors, passenger and train conductors.

AHOY, MATE!

Movement of huge amounts of cargo, as well as passengers, between nations and within our nation depends on workers in water transportation occupations. They operate and maintain deep sea merchant ships, tugboats, towboats, ferries, dredges, excursion vessels, and other waterborne craft.

WIDE ANGLE

At-A-Glance

Education:

Commercial Airline Pilots: Be at least 23 years old, have a minimum of 1,500 hours of flight experience (including night and instrument flying), have an airline transport pilot's license, have advanced **FAA** ratings, passage of psychological and aptitude tests.

Helicopter Pilots: Be at least 18 years old, have 250 hours of flight experience, and have a commercial pilot's certificate with a helicopter rating.

Air Traffic Controller: Three years general work experience, four-year degree, or combination of both; passage of week-long screening tests conducted at **FAA** Academy.

Airline Attendant: Be at least 19 years old, have completed four to six weeks of intensive training at an airlines' flight training center.

Railroad Transportation Workers: A high school diploma. Railroad transportation workers usually begin as yard laborers, and later be trained for engineer or conductor jobs.

Water Transportation Workers: Be licensed by the U.S. Coast Guard, which offers different licenses, depending on the position and type of craft.

Deck or Engineering Officers: Graduate of U.S. Merchant Marine Academy or one of the six state academies; passage of written examination.

Outlook:

Slower-than-average growth in all but airline industry.

Earnings:

Commercial airline pilot:	$15,000-$200,000+
Commercial helicopter pilot:	$33,700-$59,900+
Corporate helicopter pilot:	$47,900-$72,500+
Air Traffic Controller:	$29,600-$46,000
Airline Attendant:	$12,800-$40,000
Rail engineer:	$52,903-$65,374
Rail Conductor:	$48,991-$62,169
Rail Operators:	$41,968-$54,448
Water Transportation Worker:	$14,924-$60,164
Captain & Mate:	$14,300-$62,556
Seamen:	$14,976-$51,116

INDEX

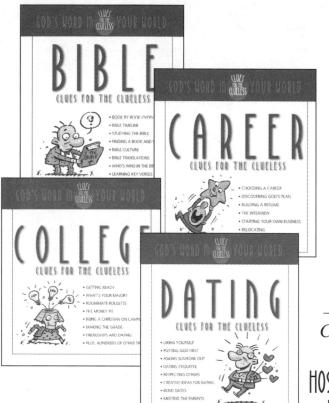